A History of the BHOPAL STATE

Glimpses of Changing Times

A History of the BHOPAL STATE

Glimpses of Changing Times

Dr. Rajeev Uberoi
and
INTACH Bhopal Chapter

INTACH BHOPAL

AMARYLLIS
An imprint of
Manjul Publishing House Pvt. Ltd.

AMARYLLIS

An imprint of Manjul Publishing House Pvt. Ltd.
• C-16, Sector 3, Noida, Uttar Pradesh 201301, India
Website: www.manjulindia.com
Registered Office:
• 2nd Floor, Usha Preet Complex,
42, Malviya Nagar, Bhopal 462 003 - India
Distribution Centres
Ahmedabad, Bengaluru, Chennai, Hyderabad,
Kochi, Kolkata, Mumbai, Noida, Pune

A History of the Bhopal State: Glimpses of Changing Times
by Dr. Rajeev Uberoi and INTACH Bhopal

This edition first published in 2025

ISBN 978-93-5543-800-3

Printed and bound in India by Parksons Graphics Pvt. Ltd.

FOREWORD

Bhopal, the capital city of Madhya Pradesh, is a very popular city in modern-day India because of its central location. Everyone going from north to south or east to west has to pass through this city. To an outsider, the introduction of Bhopal is largely confined to being called the City of Lakes and the city loves to be called this. This name shows its the closeness to nature which bestows a rich natural environment to it.

The city derives its name from the legendary Raja Bhoj, who belonged to the Parmar dynasty and controlled a huge part of present-day Madhya Pradesh. At its peak, it extended into Rajasthan, Gujarat, and parts of Maharashtra.

There are very few well-researched books written about the important phases in the history of the Bhopal state. Significant historical records have been lost because of poor record-keeping owing to the lack of proper archiving systems during the Nawab era. Added to this is the complexity that all records of the Nawab era are in the Persian language which is neither taught to nor understood by the present generation. It's a Herculean task today to get a good translation of a Persian government record done into English or Hindi. There are very few books written in English by some Englishmen during the 18th to 20th centuries CE, that talk about the state of affairs in the Bhopal state.

Bhopal city remained prime focus in the time of its erstwhile statehood, and each generation of rulers and their associates left some imprint on the fabric of time. Due to neglect by the ruling families and issues of inheritance, Bhopal has suffered significant damages to its built or architectural heritage. Poor protection, lack of awareness about conservation, and commitment to protection of heritage buildings by those who own such historically significant properties have remained a major concern for heritage lovers.

INTACH Bhopal Chapter has tried to write about significant monuments built during the period between 1709 CE to 1949 CE. Some narratives have been built around the heritage buildings seen on the ground. The Britishers, after the Treaty of 1818 (known as the Treaty of Raisen), became the true controllers of military and administrative powers in the region. A permanent British resident was also positioned at Bhopal to ensure that the provisions of the treaty were strictly enforced. Therefore, the next 130 years were the years of British rule, with limited powers given to the Nawab in important matters. The real story of the short or the long rule of a Nawab or Begum will need very extensive and comprehensive research using the vast resources of the National Archives at Bhopal, the British Museum in New Delhi and the records of Maratha rulers at Pune, but that will be another project we can aspire to take up.

This book will give useful links into the times of the Bhopal State and will give many leads to the readers to further explore history and get new insights.

INTACH Bhopal Chapter has tried to get as much information as possible using all the possible resources that are available, but the limitation of very poor record-keeping had been a handicap. This may improve in the times to come.

17th November, 2024
Bhopal

Madan Mohan Upadhyay,
Convenor,
INTACH Bhopal Chapter.

PREFACE

Bhopal, with its modernity and rapid growth, has transformed into the city of dreams, luring people with its moderate climate and lush green landscapes. Yet, beneath its contemporary facade lies a treasure trove of history, etched into the monuments that have withstood the test of time. This book is a labour of love, an endeavour to unveil Bhopal's monumental architectural heritage-a rich tapestry of styles and influences forged through interactions with diverse traditions.

The early architectural footprints date back to the 11th century CE when the Paramara Dynasty, under the patronage of Raja Bhoja and later Udayaditya Parmara, made the first attempt to establish a township here. However, it was during the reign of the Nawabs of Bhopal that the city truly began to flourish. In its infancy, the state grappled with conflicts and territorial disputes, diverting attention away from its architectural legacy. It wasn't until 1819, when Bhopal secured a treaty with the British, that external threats subsided, affording the rulers the luxury to nurture their city's cultural and architectural essence.

Bhopal's historical legacy, including the remarkable contributions of its Begums and Nawabs, remains relatively obscure in the annals of history. The city boasts a diverse heritage—a cultural mosaic interwoven with monuments and history. It is imperative that this invaluable heritage be made accessible and shared with both current and future generations. These monuments are not mere relics of the past; they are living witnesses to our history, culture, and identity. They are the legacy we must earnestly strive to pass on to the future. The dissemination of this knowledge fosters pride in one's heritage.

This book serves as a unique portal into Bhopal's history, predominantly through the prism of its monuments and heritage. It dives deep into the historical context, spotlighting the rulers who played pivotal roles in shaping this legacy and offering insights into the monuments themselves. Amidst the celebration of our rich heritage, it is impossible to ignore the distressing reality that many of these architectural gems languish in a state of neglect and disrepair. This book, therefore, is a plea to rekindle interest in these treasures left behind by our forebears—a call to witness, appreciate, utilise, and preserve them for future generations. Sadly, we have thus far fallen short in these responsibilities. It is a painful truth that some of our cherished heritage sites are in deplorable condition. This predicament necessitates a collective awakening—a recognition of the dire straits our heritage faces. It demands a unified effort involving residents, civil society, administration, and the state to embark on a mission of restoration and preservation. It is incumbent upon us and future generations not only to take pride in these invaluable heirlooms but also to actively participate in their restoration and ongoing upkeep.

Bhopal holds a special place in my heart; it's the city I hold most dear. Though my formative years saw me depart for schooling in 1969 CE, my connection with the city has never wavered. This document represents my humble effort to give back to Bhopal and its residents by providing insights into their heritage and past. While not exhaustive, it serves as a modest starting point-a spark I hope will ignite countless others worldwide who share roots and affiliations with this remarkable, hospitable, beautiful, and welcoming city to continue and expand upon this vital initiative. Together, we can ensure that Bhopal's rich history and cultural significance remain alive and celebrated for generations to come.

Safeguarding our heritage is 'an ode to the past,' 'a present to the present,' and 'an investment in the future.'

Rajeev Uberoi

(Rajeev Uberoi)

CONTENTS

01

BHOPAL: PRIOR TO THE NAWABS

The Bhopal region, in ancient times, fell within the bounds of the Avanti Janapada. Subsequently, the Nanda dynasty held sway over this territory, followed by Chandragupta Maurya, the founding figure of the Mauryan dynasty, who assumed control from the 4th century BCE onward.

The history of mankind dates back to the Stone Age or even before. Bhopal, due to its location, has witnessed human existence on its natural canvas since the Stone Age. The evidence for this can be seen in the hand tools dating back to the same era, discovered at different sites in the city of Bhopal[1]. Our prehistoric ancestors roamed the slopes of Dharmapuri, Shyamla Hills[2] and Lalghati bordering the Bada Talab.[3,4] Painted rock shelters in the Lalghati area date back to the Mesolithic period.[5] These regions' cave paintings and rock shelters are proof that people once lived there.[6] Due to increased quarrying and construction activities, majority of the rock paintings have been fully or partially destroyed. After the Bronze age, the historical record of this region became increasingly obscure. Tangible historical evidence emerges from the 6th century BCE onwards, a period during which 16 distinct Mahajanapadas emerged in the Indian subcontinent. The Bhopal region, during this time, fell within the bounds of the Avanti Janapada. Subsequently, the Nanda dynasty held sway over this territory, followed by Chandragupta Maurya, the founding figure of the Mauryan dynasty, who assumed control from the 4th century BCE onward. Notable remnants of this epoch can be traced back to the reign of Ashoka, an adherent of Buddhism. Within this region, one can discover stupas of varying sizes, with the Sanchi Stupa group standing out as the most prominent example.

Following the illustrious reign of the Mauryas, several other dynasties took their turn, including the Shungas, Satvahanaas, Kushanas, Shakyas, Nagas, among others, prior to the ascendancy of the Guptas as the dominant ruling dynasty. Starting in the 4th century CE, the Guptas began their rule in this region, substantiated by archaeological findings at sites like Sanchi and the Udaygiri caves.

After the decline of Guptas, it came under the control of the Hunas. Subsequently, during the 7th century CE, the Thaneshwar clan established their rule in this area. However, historical records become scarcer regarding the ruling clan in this area after this period. From the latter half of the 8th century until the first half of the 9th century CE, the Gurjara Pratiharas emerged as prominent rulers in the Malwa region, incorporating the region of Bhopal into their dominion. Following the Gurjara Pratiharas, the Parmaras governed this area as allies of the Rashtrakutas.

Bhopal was founded by the Parmar ruler, Raja Bhoj in 1010–1053 CE. The earlier name of the city was 'Bhojpal', which was derived from the treaty of Bhoj and Pal.[7] During the reign of King Bhoja, Bhopal probably acted as an important guardian city to the water body *Bada Talab. Bojapala,* a fortified gridiron city, was situated to the east of the lake. Over the dam that contained the lake was a small fortification called *Kila Kohna.* In *Bhojapala,* there also existed a gurukul, or place of learning, called *Sabha Mandala.* This was probably built in 1184 CE by Rani Salmali, wife of the grandson of King Bhoja. The Sabha

Mandala complex was ruined and the city of Bhopal Tal was ravaged when Sultan Iltutmish attacked and plundered Malwa in 1236 CE.[8]

In the beginning of the 14th century, a Gond warrior called Yadoram established Gondwana, the mighty Gond Kingdom, with his headquarters at Garha Mandla. The Gond dynasty had a number of powerful kings like Madan Shah, Gorakhdas, Arjundas, and Sangram Shah. During the Mughal invasion of Malwa, a sizable area of the territory comprising Bhopal state was under the possession of the Gond Kingdom. These territories were known as Chaklas,of which *Chakla* Ginnour was one, consisting of 750 villages. Bhopal was a part of it. The Gond king Nizam Shah, son of Suraj Singh Shah, was the ruler of this area.[9]

He was married to Princess Kamlapati, daughter of Raja Kripal Singh Sarautua of Salkanpur, Sehore. Rani Kamlapati, known for her intelligence and courage, was an expert horse rider, wrestler, and archer. As a skilled general, she and her battalion fought in battles alongside her father and his military.[10] She was the seventh and favourite wife of King Nizam Shah. King Nizam Shah built a seven-storied palace in Bhopal as a token of his love for the queen in 1700 CE. Rani Kamlapati and her husband used to work together on state projects, including comprehending the needs of the populace, paying attention to the Gond culture of the state, and maintaining financial records for the government. The advancement of Ginnaurgarh and the beauty of the queen began to surprise the rulers in the region. Alam Shah, the princely monarch of Bari, was the nephew of Nizam Shah and resided in the vicinity of Ginnaurgarh. A disagreement over the state had also developed between the Nizam Shah and his nephew. Alam Shah wished to take over the territory of his uncle.[11]

Nizam Shah met his demise due to poisoning, allegedly orchestrated by Alam Shah. Afterward, Alam Shah redirected his focus towards the kingdom ruled by Rani Kamlapati. Concerned for their safety, Rani Kamlapati and her son, Naval Shah, relocated from Ginnaurgarh to the Kamlapati palace in Bhopal. Naval Shah was still a minor at that time.

Following Nizam Shah's death, Rani Kamlapati reached an agreement with Dost Mohammed Khan to govern the state's affairs. Dost Mohammed Khan, a shrewd and cunning Afghan sardar, began consolidating power by annexing smaller principalities. Upon Rani Kamlapati's passing, Dost Mohammed Khan seized the fort of Ginnaurgarh, quelled rebellions, distributed grants based on control to other leaders, and garnered their gratitude. This marked the beginning of the intriguing history of the Nawabs of Bhopal.[12]

The Bhimbetka Rock Shelters, located in the foothills of the Vindhya Range in central India, stand as a testament to the rich history of human habitation and artistic expression in the region. Discovered in 1957 CE by the renowned archaeologist Dr. Vishnu Shridhar Wakankar,, these natural rock shelters, situated approximately 45 kilometer south of Bhopal, within the Ratapani Wildlife Sanctuary in west-central Madhya Pradesh, have captivated the world with their archaeological significance and stunning collection of prehistoric art. With over 700 shelters, Bhimbetka is one of the largest repositories of ancient art, and its importance is underscored by its designation as a UNESCO World Heritage site in 2003 CE.[13]

The Bhimbetka region is characterised by sandstone rock formations that have been weathered over time, creating a unique landscape that served as a canvas for prehistoric artists. The archaeological exploration of the site has been particularly focused on a hill within the complex, where 243 shelters have been investigated. Of these, 133 shelters contain remarkable rock paintings that showcase narrative skill and a vivid depiction of various aspects of prehistoric life.[14]

The art found within the Bhimbetka Rock Shelters is categorised into different periods of prehistory, each revealing insights into the evolving cultural and social dynamics of early human societies. The oldest paintings, dating back to the Late Paleolithic Period (Old Stone Age), present large linear representations of animals like rhinoceroses and bears, reflecting the interactions and observations of the early inhabitants with their environment. As the timeline progresses, the art transitions into the Mesolithic Period (Middle Stone Age), where smaller paintings depict both animals and human activities, providing glimpses into the daily lives of these ancient people.[15] Moving further through time, the Chalcolithic Period (early Bronze age) paintings reveal the early humans' evolving conceptions of agriculture and settlement practices. The artistic expressions from this period hint at the transition from nomadic hunter-gatherer societies to more settled agrarian communities. Lastly, the rock paintings from early historical times unveil a fascinating array of religious motifs, including depictions of tree gods and magical sky chariots, offering insights into the spiritual beliefs and practices of the people who inhabited the region.[16]

The Bhimbetka Rock Shelters offer a rare and invaluable window into the sequence of cultural development that spans from the early days of nomadic hunter-gatherer societies to the emergence of settled agricultural communities and the subsequent expressions of spirituality. Interestingly, the present-day cultural traditions of the villagers living in the twenty-one adjacent villages exhibit remarkable similarities to those depicted in the ancient rock paintings. This continuity between past and present underscores the enduring influence of these prehistoric societies on the cultural fabric of the region.

The Sanchi Stupa stands as one of India's oldest stone structures and a significant monument of Indian architecture. Situated in a plateau region just west of the Betwa River, approximately 8 kilometers southwest of Vidisha in Madhya Pradesh, was originally commissioned by the Mauryan emperor Ashoka the Great in the 3rd century BCE.

Sanchi Stupa

The great stupa was initially made of bricks and featured a simple hemispherical structure built over the Buddha's relics. At its summit, a chhatra, resembling a parasol, symbolised high rank and served to honour and shelter the sacred remains.[17]

In the 1st century BCE, four intricately carved toranas (ornamental gateways) and a balustrade were added to the structure during the Shunga period. The toranas of the Great Stupa are an extraordinary achievement of Sanchi sculpture. Each gateway comprises two squared posts with sculpted animal or dwarf capitals, topped by three architraves. The exquisite proportions and elaborate sculpted decorations make Stupa 1 a remarkable artistic masterpiece.[18]

Several temples were also constructed at Sanchi during different periods, including Temple 40, a 3rd-century BCE structure contemporaneous with the core of the Great Stupa, and the Gupta Temple no. 18, etc.[19]

Over time, the site of Sanchi faced various changes and deterioration. It flourished until the 11th century CE, after which it was abandoned and fell into disrepair. In 1818 CE, British General Henry Taylor stumbled upon the site and documented his findings.[20] Restoration efforts commenced in 1881 CE and were completed in 1919 CE, under the supervision of John Hubert Marshall, the director-general of the Indian Archaeological Survey. The stupas at Sanchi (numbered 1, 2, and 3) were restored in the early 20th century CE, preserving the original features characteristic of mature stupas.

It is well-known that Sultan Jahan Begum and her mother provided significant financial support for the preservation and conservation of the ancient Buddhist Stupa at Sanchi. John Marshall, the Director-General of the Archaeological Survey of India from 1902 to 1928 CE, gratefully acknowledged her generous donations by dedicating his important volume, "A Guide to Sanchi," to Begum Sultan Jahan. Moreover, Sultan Jahan played a pivotal role in funding the construction of the Archaeological Museum at Sanchi in 1919 CE, which subsequently came to be known as the Sanchi Museum.[21]

The Mauryan Pillar in Bagh Umrao Dulha, Bhopal, is a magnificent testament to the city's ancient history. This circular monolithic pillar, made of polished sandstone, predates the Nawabi era of Bhopal. Adorned with an inverted lotus and open lotus leaf capital, it showcases remarkable craftsmanship. Inscribed with undeciphered Shankh Lipi (script), its origins remain debated, possibly dating back to the Mauryan or Gupta era. The pillar's enigmatic inscriptions and its true age continue to intrigue historians, leaving room for further exploration.

It Has been brought to its current location by one of the Begum of Bhopal within the Tranquil Bagh. Hence it also got the name Umrao Dulha Pillar. During the plague outbreak in 1918 CE, the Bagh Umrao Dulha served as a quarantine, and Begum Sultan Jahan sought solace there.

Udayagiri Caves, located approximately 6.5 km from Vidisha, Madhya Pradesh, is a cave complex with a history dating back to the 5th century CE. Comprising 20 rock-cut caves, this site holds significant Hindu and Jain iconography. Protected by the Archaeological Survey of India, these caves were excavated during the reign of Chandragupta II and bear Brahmi inscriptions as evidence.

The caves are adorned with exquisite sculptures depicting tales of gods and goddesses. Notably, Cave 5, known as the Varaha Cave, showcases Vishnu's incarnation as a boar rescuing the Earth Goddess, Prithvi. Cave 6 features fine carvings of deities like Ganesha, Vishnu, Shiva, Brahma, Shakti Durga, and Mahishasura Mardini. A captivating sight is the 12-ft long reclining Vishnu in one of the caves, displaying exceptional artistic craftsmanship.[22]

Numerous inscriptions found in the caves provide valuable information about their origin and significance. Cave 7's Sanskrit inscriptions link it to 5th-century CE Shaivism, while a Jain devotee's inscription in Cave 20 reflects the influence of Jainism. Despite their complexity, caves portray the skilled craftsmanship involved in carving these caves out of rock. From a distance, the area appears to be a typical forested landscape, concealing the priceless history within its beautifully sculpted caves.[23]

Bhojpur Temple, also known as the Somnath of the East, stands on the banks of the Betwa River in Raisen district. It was founded by King Bhoj in the early mediaeval period and is dedicated to Lord Shiva. The temple's history dates back to 1010 CE when Raja Bhoj ordered its construction. However, the temple remained incomplete, and today, the Archaeological Survey of India takes care of its maintenance and completion.

The architectural features of the Bhojpur Temple are fascinating, with unique aspects like the absence of a Mandapa attached to the Garbhagriha and the use of a rectilinear roof instead of the traditional curved Shikhara. The temple's entry wall is adorned with engravings of pillar patterns and bells.

The main attraction of the temple is the 7.5-foot-tall stone Shivling placed on a 21-foot-tall platform. The shivling is about 18 feet in circumference and is made up of three limestone blocks stacked on top of each other. An iron stairway leads to the sanctum, facilitating easy worship rituals for the devotees. The temple is supported by four pillars, and the massive stone dome reaches a height of 40 feet. Stone

Bhojpur Temple

carvings adorn the dome, facade, and pillars of the temple, adding to its grandeur.[24]

Originally, the temple was located on the banks of a reservoir, which was 29.8 kilometer long and 12.1 kilometer wide. Raja Bhoj constructed three stone-based dams to create this reservoir. However, the artificial reservoir was drained in the 15th century CE when two of the dams were broken. In 2015 CE, the temple received the National Tourism Award for being the 'Best Maintained and Disabled Friendly Monument.' The temple attracts numerous visitors, especially during Maha Shivaratri, and hosts the annual Bhojpur Utsava, a cultural event celebrated around the auspicious occasion.

Ashapuri is a remarkable archaeological site featuring 26 temples in ruins, nestled closely together on the slopes of a rocky hillock, only 6 kms away from Bhojpur Shiva Temple. This sacred complex was once surrounded by dense forests and flowing waters, and its construction spanned over two centuries between the ninth and eleventh centuries, with patronage from the Pratiharas and Parmaras dynasties in central India.

As time passed, the fortunes of the site changed, leading to decline due to changing dynasties, scarcity of funds, natural disasters, and invasions. In the past, master architects and their young apprentices would sculpt stone temples while chanting hymns and reciting Sanskrit texts on temple construction. The atmosphere would have been filled with music from the wind, water, hymns, and the sound of chiselling stones. However, temples fell into disrepair, and the site remained hidden under the earth for centuries until the Department of Archaeology and Museums, Madhya Pradesh, launched an excavation program in 2010 CE. With the support of the World Monuments Fund, the Ashapuri Temple Project began, involving collaboration between the Welsh School of Architecture, Cardiff University, and the School of Planning and Architecture, Bhopal.

The project aims to document, reconstruct, and preserve the temple site, providing a unique opportunity to understand ancient Indian temple design and construction methods. With proper arrangement and conservation efforts, Ashapuri has the potential to become an exceptional place for studying ancient temple architecture in India. WMF's partnership with the government of Madhya Pradesh's

Department of Culture ensures the development of a sustainable management program for the preservation of the state's heritage sites.[25]

Bada Talab, also known as Upper Lake, holds historical significance in the city of Bhopal, which is believed to have been founded by Parmar Raja Bhoj in the 11th century CE. Formerly known as Bhojtal, it serves as a significant source of drinking water, supplying approximately 40% of the city's residents with around 30 million imperial gallons of water daily. Surrounded by Van Vihar National Park on the south, human settlements on the east and north, and agricultural fields on the west, Bhojtal has an area of 31 km square and drains a catchment or watershed of 361 km square. The lake was formed by constructing an earthen dam and a diversion channel, causing the upper reach of the Kolans River and Bada Talab to now drain into the Kaliasot River.

The Bada Talab area encompassed a vast dam structure, approximately 1 km long, located about 4 km before Bhojpur temple on the Misrod Chiklod road. There is also a smaller dam, around 500 metres from Bhojpur Temple, measuring approximately 100 metres in length and 15 metres in height. Collectively, these embankments covered a dam area of around 250 square miles.[26]

According to the legend, Raja Bhoj suffered from a skin disease. His religious scholars advised him to unite nine rivers and 99 streams at one place, take a bath in them, distribute charity, and seek blessings from 99 Brahmins to cure his ailment. The wise minister, Kalyan Singh, managed to bring water from the Betwa River and its tributaries, along with a river from Bhojtal, forming a large dam named "BHIM KUND." Raja Bhoj performed the holy bath and developed the village of Bhojpur near this dam.[27] It was once lined with several ghats, one of which was the Purana Ghat. This ghat, hidden beneath the waters until 2002 CE when the water level receded, was constructed using large, untreated blocks of Sandstone around the 17th century CE. Having been in existence since the 11th century CE, Bhopal city has developed around Bhojtal, and the local community holds religious and cultural significance for the lake.

Bhojtal has been a recognised Ramsar site since 2002 CE under the Ramsar Convention of 1971 CE. It is the only man-made lake to be in this list. The lake faces challenges such as permanent developments on its wetland, shrinkage and pollution due to human activities. NGT

(National Green Tribunal) keeps a check on it to avoid any ecological harm to the lake and flora and fauna flourishing around it.

Mata Mandir, an ancient structure predating the Nawabs era, stands near Bada Talab. Enclosed within a walled building, this magnificent Islamic-style temple with a dome as its shikhara is truly mesmerising to behold. The temple's entrance is adorned with double arches, the outer one being cusped and the inner one pointed. A stone jharokha-like projection crowns the top of its facade. The main entrance of the temple, featuring Bangaldhar-style roofing, currently opens into the lake, with narrow steps leading down to the gateway. Inside the compound, two chhatri-like temples of intricately carved stone add to its sacred aura.

There are ghats descending from the temple to the lake, known as Pucca Ghat, made of red sandstone tiles, and regularly maintained with public donations. The compound wall is adorned with elaborate moulded coping and crenellations facing Bada Talab. On the talab side wall, two impressive pavilions with onion-shaped domes and carved stone pillars flank the temple. While the exact date of its creation remains uncertain, it is believed to have been built around the seventeenth century CE.

Situated in Shehr-e-Khas, this temple is devoted to Krishna and belongs to the Vallabh Sampradaya, a sect that emphasises Seva (service) over worship. The temple's architectural style resembles that of a house, featuring a spacious entrance gate leading to a double-height hall. On the opposite side of the hall lies the Garbhagriha, and its door shutters are adorned with silver sheets. The temple boasts various architectural elements like carved stone pillars, stone brackets, stone jalis, and cusped arches. According to folklore, during Janmashtami, the begums partook in a joyous celebration at the temple, dancing in Hindu attire, the Saree. On this special occasion, the begum received offerings as Prasad in the pallu of her saree.

Garhi Khanugaon stands at Khanugaon, opposite Noor-us-Sabah, representing the majestic architecture of the Gond civilization. This small fortress, built with precision, spans an area of 180 m by 150 m, facing the east. Four sturdy bastions adorn its corners, and the sole entrance is located at the centre of the eastern side. Legend has it that the four peers who accompanied Nawab Dost Mohammad Khan settled within these bastions upon their arrival in Bhopal. The garhi's defensive wall, constructed with a thickness of 1.5 m using rubble masonry, rises to a formidable height of 4 m. The entrance gate, still intact, features a timber gateway within a larger arched opening. A lintel has been inserted, creating a smaller rectangular opening. While further historical details are scarce, Garhi Khanugaon and its surroundings offer glimpses into the past of the region before the establishment of Bhopal State.

In the 17th century CE, Mangalgarh was a small Rajput principality ruled by Raja Anand Singh Solanki. The principality received protection from the Pathan mercenary, Dost Mohammad Khan. Dost Mohammad earned favour with the dowager mother of the Raja, and after the Raja's demise, she appointed him as the mukhtar (guardian) of Mangalgarh around 1708 CE. Dost's main responsibility was to protect the dowager Rani and her estate.

When the neighbouring Rajput rulers of Mangalgarh, led by the Thakur of Parason (now a village in Berasia tehsil), formed an alliance to counter the growing influence and power of the Rani of Mangalgarh, Dost Mohammad Khan took decisive action and defeated them in battle.

During his service in Mangalgarh, Dost Mohammad Khan married a Rajput girl from the Mangalgarh royal family. She later converted to Islam and adopted the name Fateh Bibi. After the heirless Rani's passing, Dost Mohammad Khan seized control of the principality, effectively making it a part of his expanding Bhopal State. Mangalgarh, which was once a jagir (land grant) in Nazirabad tehsil, became integrated into the Bhopal State under Dost Mohammad Khan's rule.[28]

The history of Raisen and its fort is a tale of shifting rulers and empires. From its early days during the Hindu times, Raisen was an important centre of administration. In the fifteenth century, the fort came under the rule of the Sultans of Mandu before passing to the Rajputs. During the Mughal period, Raisen served as the headquarters of a Sarkar in the Subah of Ujjain in Malwa.[29] It changed hands again and was eventually occupied by Fiaz Mohammad Khan, the third Nawab of Bhopal State, who declared himself the Faujdar of Raisen under Emperor Alamgir II. The fort has witnessed various historical events, including its capture by Shershah Suri in 1543 CE during the

Raisen Fort

reign of Akbar. Over time, different parts of the region served as the headquarters of various areas, such as Khamkhera, Shahpur, and Sagoni.[30]

Raisen holds a significant historical and cultural heritage in the form of the Raisen Fort. The Raisen Fort is perched on top of a hill, boasting several temples, palaces, a large water reservoir, and numerous wells inside its complex. With a history spanning approximately 800 years, the fort occupies the entire hilltop and showcases the architectural marvels of its time. While the fort once housed many domes, only two of them remain today, now serving as the habitat of bats.[31]

Besides the Raisen Fort, the area is renowned for the Dargah of Hazrat Peer Fatehullah Shah Baba, a revered Muslim saint. The shrine holds deep spiritual significance for the local community, and it is believed that the saint's blessings can fulfil the desires of pilgrims.

The name "Raisen" is believed to be a corruption of Rajavasini or Rajasayan, suggesting a connection to a royal residence. This name is closely associated with the massive Raisen Fort, which stands as a testament to the region's history and royal heritage. In more recent times, after India gained independence, Raisen became the headquarters of the newly formed district on May 5, 1950 CE.

Hoshangabad Fort, situated on the banks of the Narmada River in Hoshangabad, holds a historical significance dating back to the 15th century CE. It was built by Sultan Hoshangshah of Malwa during the first half of the 15th century CE. The foundation of both the fort and the city was laid by Sultan Hoshangshah, giving rise to the name "Hoshangabad" in his honour. The fort covers an area of approximately eight acres. The walls of the Hoshangabad Fort are adorned with arch formations and Kanguras, reflecting the architectural brilliance of its time. However, today, only one bastion and a 1.25-meter thick, 5-6 metre high security wall, along with the passage leading to the bastion and a security post room, remain.Much of the original fort has eroded over time.

Over time, the fort underwent various modifications and reconstructions. In the 18th century, it was expanded and reconstructed to its present form. The fort played a role in military expeditions, as it was used by the ruler of Khedala, located in present-day Betul district, to conduct expeditions against the ruler of Bahamani. The fort has witnessed several historical events, and local beliefs suggest that Sultan Hoshangshah himself died in Hoshangabad, with his grave located within the fort's premises.

Throughout history, Hoshangabad and the surrounding region experienced changes in rulership. After the fall of the Mughal Empire, the area was divided into multiple political divisions, with different rulers controlling various parts of the district. Ultimately, the territories of Ginnaurgarh, including the Hoshangabad Fort, came under the rule of Dost Mohammad Khan in 1722 CE. Later, the region came under the control of the Bhonsla Raja of Nagpur.

In the 19th century CE, the British East India Company occupied Hoshangabad during the Anglo-Maratha war. It was subsequently ceded to the British, and the district's territories were consolidated under the title "Saugor and Nerbudda Territories" in 1820 CE. In recent times, the district's name was changed from "Hoshangabad" to "Narmadapuram" on February 7, 2022 CE.

Ichhawar was a town located in the Nizamat-i-Maghrib, the western district of Bhopal State. Situated at 23° 2' N. and 77° 1' E. The town was established on the foundations of the village of Lakshmipura. It was fortified by the Marathas in 1716 CE and later came under the control of Bhopal State through the treaty of 1818 CE.[32]

The Ichhawar tehsil was held as a jagir by the Bhopal Bourbons for many years, contributing shrewd counsellors and valiant soldiers to the State. The Bourbon family has a fascinating history, tracing back to Jean Philippe Bourbon of Navarre, a cousin of Henry IV, who arrived in India around 1560 CE. He served under Akbar and married Juliana, rumoured to be a sister of Akbar's 'Christian wife,' and thus, becoming a Nawab.

Following the ransacking of Delhi by Nadir Shah in 1739 CE, the Bourbon family sought refuge in the fort of Shergarh (25° 35' N. and 77° 58' E.) within the territory of the Narwar chief. In 1778 CE, the Raja of Narwar attacked Shergarh, resulting in a massacre, but four members of the family managed to escape to Gwalior. Subsequently, they were granted territory after the capture of Gwalior in 1780 CE, with Salvador Bourbon serving in the Bhopal State's army as a general.

Balthasar, the son of Salvador Bourbon, acted as a minister to Wazir Muhammad and played a crucial role in the signing of the treaty of 1818 CE with the British Government. During the Mutiny of 1857 CE, Jean de Silva and several Bourbon family members residing in the town extended hospitality to the fleeing individuals from Agar. Even today, descendants of the Bourbon family continue to reside in the State. The history of Ichhawar is thus intertwined with the rich legacy of the Bhopal Bourbons and their significant contributions to the region.

Kurwai State, situated in British India and falling under the jurisdiction of the Bhopal Agency, was centred around the town of Kurwai. This princely state, encompassing an area of 368 square kilometres, had its origins in the year 1713 CE when it was established by Mohammed Diler Khan, an Afghan soldier serving in the Mughal army. The foundation of the town of Kurwai took place in 1715 CE.[33]

During the 1730s CE, Kurwai State came under the suzerainty of the Maratha Empire. However, in 1818 CE, after the British emerged victorious in the Third Anglo-Maratha War, Kurwai transitioned into a British protectorate. This shift marked its formal inclusion under British authority.[34]

Positioned on the eastern side of the town, Kurwai Fort was constructed from abundant gneiss rock found in the vicinity. It is located along the right bank of the Betwa River and is situated atop a slight elevation.[35] The construction of fort was commissioned by Nawab Diler Mohammad Khan. Nawab Diler Khan, a cousin of Nawab Dost Mohammad Khan of Bhopal, received the fort as a gift from his uncle during military campaigns.[36]

Over the years, Kurwai Fort witnessed the reign of several Nawabs, including Nawab Najaf Mohammad Khan (1822-1887 CE), Nawab Munawwar Ali Khan (1869-1896 CE), and Nawab Yaqub Ali Khan (1876-1906 CE). Each ruler contributed to the fort's legacy during their time in power.

The ruler of Kurwai State undertook the process of acceding to the Dominion of India on 15 June 1948 CE. This significant step signalled the conclusion of Kurwai's independent status, leading to its integration into the newly formed Indian nation.[37]

One noteworthy historical aspect of the fort is its association with the birthplace of Shaharyar Khan, who later became the Chairman of the Pakistan Cricket Board. Born in the grand Kothis of the Kurwai Fort, Shaharyar Khan also served as the 20th Foreign Secretary of Pakistan from 1990 to 1994 CE.

Despite India gaining independence and Kurwai merging with the nation, the descendants of Nawab Sarwar Ali Khan continue to reside in the fort.[38]

Ginnorgarh Fort, located approximately 60 km from Bhopal, is a remarkable historical relic situated on a hill 3 km from Delawadi. Spanning 1230 yards in length and 150 yards in breadth at coordinates 22° 49' N. and 77V° 36' E. It comes under the forest area of Ratapani Wildlife Sanctuary. The fort is referred to as "Gunnora " in the Bhopal plates of Udayvarma Parmara dating back to 1200 CE.[39]

Ginnorgarh Hill Fort is not only picturesque but is an architectural marvel too. The fortress is situated atop a solitary hill, encompassed by a series of low hills, granting it inherent protection against invaders. During their reign, the Gonds fortified the walls of the fort, which stretched across a length of 1127 metres and breadth of 266 metres. The fort's layout is irregular, with deep ravines encircling it on all sides, offering an added layer of security. Strategically placed along the fortification wall, bastions were built, with the main gate housing larger bastions that served as storage for grain and provided enhanced defence compared to the others.

Within the fort, there were wells, tanks, tombs, and a small yet exquisite palace designed in the Mughal style. Unfortunately, the palace was demolished, and its materials were repurposed to construct another building within the premises. On the western side of the fort, there were opulent structures, one of which, a two-story edifice, remains intact to this day.

It has at least eight different Baolis atop the hill and a few water tanks spread around at the foothill, including two natural water bodies. Within the dilapidated walls of the fort, remnants of grand domes and Baolis (stepwells) can still be observed. Majority of the water structures are deteriorating.

The fort is comprised of six gateways, among them is the main entrance, as well as a pair of palaces known as Hawa Mahal and Rani Mahal. Additionally, several other unidentified structures can be found in the surrounding area. Of particular significance is Gate No. 3, which features a noteworthy Persian inscription. This inscription bears the information that the gateway was constructed in 1725 CE under the patronage of Nawab Yar Mohammad Khan, the second nawab of Bhopal.[40]

According to folklore, Ginnorgarh Fort was a stronghold, constructed by Gond king Bhupal Singh Salam, who supposedly lived there with his seven beautiful queens 800 years ago. As a testament to his love, Nizam Shah constructed a magnificent seven-storied palace for Queen Kamlapati in Bhopal around 1700 CE. Together, they worked diligently on state projects, served the people, preserved Gond culture, and maintained meticulous financial records.

In 1722 CE, the fort was occupied by Nizam Shah, a Gond chief, whose wife was the famous Rani Kamalapati. Subsequently, it was taken over by Dost Mohommad Khan in the 18th century CE. Over the years, Ginnorgarh Fort changed hands several times, with rulers like Nawab

Rani Kamlapati Palace

Wazir Mohammad Khan using it as a retreat during periods of local conflicts in Bhopal. Today, the fort is a popular destination for history enthusiasts and trekkers.[41]

The presence of the rulers of Bhopal at Ginnorgarh is testified by later buildings and an inscription in Persian on one of the gatehouses dated 1725-26 CE. During the reign of Sikandar Jahan Begum, daughter of Qudsia Begum, Ginnorgarh witnessed a revival. By the early twentieth century CE. Luard noted that the buildings at Ginnorgarh were falling into ruins.

In the early 18th century CE, Rani Kamlapati Palace was constructed by the last Gond queen, Rani Kamlapati, wife of the Gond king Nizam Shah. This magnificent palace, situated on the ramparts of the dam, consists of five stories and is characterised by its narrow depth. With two stories above the ground and the rest below, the palace is connected to the lower lake by a staircase. The architectural features of the palace include cusped arches, stone arches, and intricately carved stone brackets supporting the jharokhas that offer stunning views of the lake.

Kamlapati park, attached to the palace, comprises an old cannon gun. The park along with Kamlapati Palace, holds great historical significance as it is the only structure in today's Bhopal city protected and maintained by the Archaeological Survey of India (ASI).

◇◇◇◇◇◇◇◇◇◇◇◇◇◇◇◇◇◇◇◇◇◇

02

SARDAR DOST MOHAMMAD KHAN (1709-1728 CE)

The history of the Bhopal State dates from the eighteenth century CE, when Dost Mohammad Khan, an Afghan of the Mirzai Khel of the Warakzais of Tirah, obtained the pargana of Berasia in Malwa. Dost Mohammad Khan's father, Nur Mohammad, accompanied his son to India, where they arrived in AH 1109 (1696–97 CE), the thirty-seventh year of the reign of Aurangzeb. Dost Mohammad went at first to Lohari Jalalabad (Shamli district in the Indian state of Uttar

Pradesh), where a colony of his clansmen had been settled.[42] Soon after his arrival, however, he killed a man in a quarrel and, fearing that he would be arrested, fled to Delhi and attached himself to a body of imperial troops that were on their way to attack the Marathas in Malwa. On reaching Malwa, he took service under the Raja of Sitamau. Later on, he deposited such belongings as he had with the Governor of Bhilsa, Mohammad Faruk, and proceeded to hire out his services to any of the numerous petty Rajput chiefs of Malwa who were ready to pay for them. A rumour of his having been killed in a skirmish reached Mohammad Faruk, who at once seized the property left in trust with him, and Dost Mohammad, on returning soon after, was only able to recover a part.[43]

He then took service under Thakur Anand Singh Solanki of Mangalgarh. Thakur was obliged to proceed to Delhi, leaving his estate in the charge of his mother and Dost Mohammad. Thakur died in Delhi, and his mother soon after, upon which Dost Mohammad appropriated such valuables as he could and went to Berasia. Berasia was at this time held on lease by Taj Mohammad Khan, who lived in Delhi and left the management of the district to his agents. These agents were quite unable to cope with their numerous Rajput neighbours, who raided and devastated the country.

Dost Mohammad once offered to take over the district and pay Rs. 30,000 a year to Taj Mohammad Khan, an Imperial Officer. The bargain was concluded, and Dost Mohammad suddenly found himself a landed proprietor. He at once sent up to the north the members of his own family and, with their help, contrived to overawe the unruly Rajputs of Khichiwara and Umatwara and restore some sort of order. As soon as he felt his position was fairly secure, he turned his attention to the acquisition of territory. In 1715 CE, Khan ran into his first conflict with another neighbouring Rajput chief, Narsingh Rao Chauhan (also known as Narsingh Deora), who owned the fortified village of Jagdishpur near Berasia. Narsingh Deora demanded tribute from the Patel of Barkhera in Dillod, who had earlier given shelter to Dost after he fled away from the Mughal camp. Khan agreed to negotiate a treaty with Narsingh, and the two parties met at Jagdishpur, with 16 men on each side. Khan pitched a tent on the banks of the Thal River (also known as Banganga) for the meeting. After a lunch arranged by him for both parties, he stepped outside on the pretext of ordering ittar (perfume) and paan (betel leaf), which was actually a signal for Khan's hiding men to kill the Rajputs. It is said that the Thal river appeared red with the blood of the victims and was therefore renamed "Halali" river (the river of slaughter). After this incident, Khan renamed Jagdishpur to Jagadishpur, strengthened the fort, and made the place his headquarters. With Jagadishpur as the capital of Dost Mohammad Khan's state, he constructed several structures as per his needs. No better illustration of the lawlessness of the day and the decay of the central power could be given than the story of the rise of this Afghan adventurer, who in the space of a few years was able to purchase the lease of an imperial district and rise by the power of his sword alone to be the founder of a line of independent princes. His next step still further illustrates the chaotic condition of the Mughal empire. Feeling his position secure, he now determined to pay off old scores on the governor of Bhilsa and sent a strong force against that place under his brother Sher Mohammad Khan. The two armies met between the villages of Jamaldi and Bagri (23°34' N.; 77° 50' E.) near Bhilsa, and a fierce fight took place in which Sher Mohammad Khan was killed by the Mewati chief of Doraha and the Bhopal force was thrown into confusion. In the meantime, however, Dost Mohammad Khan, who had been concealed behind the hill of Bagri, came up and, suddenly surrounding Mohammad Faruk, who, with some fresh troops, was watching the fight from a distance, attacked and killed him.

Dost Mohammad Khan then mounted Mohammad Faruk's elephant and, forcing the drummers to sound the drums, marched to Bhilsa, where he was taken for Mohammad Faruk, who had returned victorious, and was at once admitted to the fort. The possession of Bhilsa made him master of the country, and Gyaraspur, Doraha, Sehore, Ichhawar, Devipura, Gulgaon, and other places soon fell into his hands.

In 1719 CE, Dost Mohammad Khan, who was on bad terms with the Nizam, joined Bhim Singh Hara of Kotah. This chief, with the help of Sayad Hussain Ali Khan, the Nizam's great rival, was marching against Rao Raja Budh Singh of Bundi, who, being an enemy of the Sayads of Barha, had been urging Chhatarsal Bundela to revolt and had also assisted Girdhar Bahadur, the rebellious Governor of Allahabad.

On 5 Muharram 1132 (17 November 1719 CE), Dost Mohammad and Bhim Singh started, with Dost Mohammad receiving a high mansab at the request of Bhim Singh. They were joined by Dilawar Ali Khan, Sayad Hussain Ali Khan's Baksi, and Raja Gaj Singh of Narwar. They defeated Budh Singh, the Kotah chief, seizing all the Bundi lands east of the Chambal.[44,45] The subahdar of Malwa Girdhar Bahadur, alarmed at the increasing power of this chief, attempted to check him but was defeated. The Governor of Shujalpur, also seeing the rising power of Dost Mohammad Khan, finally handed over that district to him, and Diler Khan, the chief of Korwai, came to pay him a complimentary visit. Their meeting was unfortunate, as a quarrel arose that resulted in the death of Diler Khan. (This, according to the Korwai annals, took place in 1134 AH or 1722 CE.) The next place of importance that fell into his hands was the fort of Ginnorgarh. Ginnorgarh was then held by a Gond chief, Nizam Shah, who had been poisoned by the chief of Chainpur Bari. Nizam Shah's widow, Rani Kamlapati, called in Dost Mohammad to assist her and her son, Newal Shah, against the poisoner. Dost Mohammad attacked the Chainpur Bari chief and annexed his territory. On Rani's death, however, he seized Ginnorgarh but treated the wives of Newal Shah with all courtesy. The last of these ladies only died at the beginning of Nawab Mohammad Hayat's time. In AH 1135, Dost Mohammad Khan, attracted by the surroundings of Bhopal, decided to build his chief town on this site, and on the 9th of Zulhijjah, AH 1135 (1722 CE), he laid the foundations of the fort of Fatehgarh. He named it after his wife, Fateh. Currently, all that remains of this fort are three bastions and a small part of the fort wall.

Jagdishpur Fort

Dost Mohammad now assumed the title of Nawab and the position of an independent chief. In 1723 CE, the Nizam, on his way to Hyderabad to quell the rebellion of his second son, Nasir Jang, entered Malwa and marched on Bhopal with the intention of dispossessing or humbling Dost Mohammad Khan. Besides the growing power of the Bhopal chief, the Nizam had an additional reason for his attack in that Dost Mohammad had assisted Dilawar Ali Khan against him in 1720 CE by sending a force under his brother, Mir Ahmad Khan, who fell by the side of Dilawar Ali Khan in the fight at Ratanpur, 30 miles from Burhanpur, on 16 Shaban 1132 AH (the 11th May CE).[46,47] The Nizam, on reaching Bhopal, encamped at a place still known as *Nizam-ki-Tekri,* near the Fort of Jagadishpur. Dost Mohammad, unable to withstand this force, made over his son Yar Mohammad Khan as a hostage, and the Nizam proceeded on his way.[48]

After thirty years of strenuous exertions, Dost Mohammad Khan, who had entered Malwa with nothing but his sword, died in AH 1139 (1726 CE) at the age of 66, leaving a well-established state behind him. The tomb of Dost Mohammad Khan stands in the fort just outside the gate leading into Bala Kila.

Dost Mohammad Khan had five brothers: Sher Mohammad Khan, killed in the fight with Mohammad Faruk; Alif Mohammad Khan, killed in the fight between Baji Rao and the Nizam; Shah Mohammad Khan, killed in a fight with Dewa Bhao, a Dhar general; Mir Ahmad Khan, killed at Burhanpur; and Akil Mohammad Khan, who was wazir of the state and was killed in a riot during Holi. Dost Mohammad Khan left six sons:

Yar Mohammad Khan (illegitimate), Sultan Mohammad Khan, Sardar Mohammad Khan, Fazil Mohammad Khan, Wasil Mohammad Khan, Khan Bahadur Khan, and five daughters.

In 1715 CE, Dost Mohommad Khan treacherously seized control of Jagdishpur by killing its local ruler, Deora Chieftain. Consequently, the village was renamed Jagadishpur and under the reign of Dost Mohammad Khan, the foundation for Islamnagar Fort was laid. Prior to the construction of Fatehgarh Fort, Islamnagar, located in the Huzur Tehsil, six miles north-west of Bhopal, served as the capital of the first Bhopal Nawab.

As the capital, Dost Mohammad Khan commissioned the construction of magnificent structures that catered to his needs and aspirations. The prominent palaces at Jagadishpur include Gond Mahal, Rani Mahal, Chaman Mahal, and Sheesh Mahal, which showcase a blend of architectural styles from Rajput, Malwa, and Mughal traditions.

Chaman Mahal was built using resplendent red sandstone and adorned with floral motifs. It featured lush gardens, enchanting fountains, and a fusion of Malwa-Mughal and Bengali architectural influences, including characteristic dropping eaves. In close proximity to the main entrance stands "Sheesh Mahal," a building adorned with painted glass-encrusted frames. Presently, it serves as a photographic museum showcasing the Afghan history of Bhopal.

Adjacent to Chaman Mahal stands Rani Mahal, a two-story zenana complex exclusively designated for the queens of Dost Mohammad Khan. Rani Mahal, meaning "Queen's Palace", serves as a dwelling specifically reserved for female residents, following the historical concept of a zenana complex. Such complexes traditionally housed the private quarters of Indian households, catering to the needs of women and encompassing courtyards, living spaces, and various amenities. These secluded quarters aimed to provide a protected environment for women to carry out their daily activities without being observed by unrelated men. In larger households, the zenana complex could be elaborate, featuring multiple buildings, gardens, and additional facilities. Women residing in these quarters typically had limited interaction with the external world and received assistance from female servants and family members.

Additionally, the palace features a colonnaded Diwan-e-Aam, a hall designated for public audiences and a Baradari. Supported by rows of columns, Diwan-e-Aam hall includes an elevated platform where the ruler or queen would be seated. This architectural aspect highlights the influence of Mughal design on the palace.

Within the fort walls, a Mughal water garden and a Turkish bath, or hamam, and antique fountains provided tranquillity. The Char Bagh garden at Jagadishpur follows the Mughal Char Bagh style and is one of the few gardens of its kind in Central India. Characterised by a symmetrical layout, it features flowering plants, fruit trees, fountains, and water channels that irrigate the flower beds with a downward flow of water. Despite being in ruins, Chaman Mahal continues to attract visitors due to its exquisite architecture and historical significance, serving as a testament to India's rich cultural heritage.

Over time, power shifted from one generation to the next, with Yar Mohammad Khan establishing Jagadishpur as his primary residence. He expanded his dominions and engaged in conflicts, including a fierce encounter with the Marathas. The fort witnessed the rise and fall of various rulers, each leaving their mark. Ghaus Mohammad, Wazir Mohammad, and Sindhia were involved in power struggles, besieging and reclaiming the fort at different points in history.

Sikandar Jahan Begum constructed numerous buildings and contributed to the reconstruction of Jagadishpur fort. Among the royal lineage, ShahJehan Begum, born in 1838 CE in Islamnagar, emerged as a prominent figure. Her birthplace provided refuge for her mother after an assassination attempt and violence of Nawab Jehangir. The fort wall with spikes on giant wooden gates at the entrance still guards the various palaces within the premises. Fortunately, the fort still stands in a considerably fine state of preservation. Recently, in Feb 2023 CE, the Madhya Pradesh government has reinstated the name of Islamnagar to Jagdishpur. The fort, along with its changing names, stands as a testament to the struggles, victories, and aspirations of the rulers who once resided within its walls.

The Kadimi Hammam, also known as Hammam-e-Kadimi, is the oldest hammam in Bhopal, still serving its purpose today. It is located across from Kamla Park and near Bada Talab. The Hammam-e-Qadimi was constructed in the early 1700s CE when the Gonds ruled the region and was later gifted to Hajjam Hammu Khalida during Dost Mohammad Khan's reign as Nawab. Designed in the style of Istanbul's Cemberlitas Hamamı, it was strategically built near a mosque to allow visitors to perform their ablutions before praying. This Indo-Turkish bath has been in the Sajid family for five generations.

The hammam is a three-chambered structure connected by a corridor. The entrance chamber features a vaulted roof with Tachas on all sides, while the other two chambers have dome roofing. However, the steam chamber is of particular significance. It uses a large copper vessel to heat water, stored in a tank above it. The heat is generated with the help of wooden logs inserted into an arched chamber. The ventilation is maintained through a complicated system known as the "ears and nose" of the building. Water was supplied from a well located beside the hammam, possibly sourced from one of the sulphur springs that Bhopal is known for.[49]

Fatehgarh Fort has an interesting story about its origin. In 1722 CE, Dost Mohammad and Fatah Bibi went on a hunting trip near Bhopal. While resting, Dost Mohammad had a dream in which a Saint advised him to build a fort. Fatah Bibi suggested that the fort be constructed at the very spot where Dost Mohammad had the dream. Kazi Mohamad Moazzam of Raisen, a renowned scholar and later appointed as the Qazi of Bhopal, laid the foundation stone with the assistance of the entire clan, including Fatah Bibi. The fort was named Fatahgarh in honour of Fatah Bibi.[50]

However, the architectural details of the fort suggest its existence before the establishment of Bhopal State by Dost Mohammad Khan. Structures like Purana Khazana and Mata Mandir near the lake indicate their presence during the Gond era. Fatehgarh Fort encompassed the village of Bhopal and eventually connected with the Old Fort of Bhopal through its ramparts. It had six gates, each named after a day of the week. The fort also featured a sun-dial, which has since been relocated to the Flagstaff House. Dost Mohammad had also acquired a Persian Quran with pages measuring five feet in length and two and a half feet in width (which was kept in this fort). This Quran was presented to the Al-Azhar University Museum in Cairo by Nawab Hamidullah Khan in 1948 CE.[51] The Fort also houses the Tomb of Sardar Dost Mohommad, whose grand vision connected Fatehgarh, Sheher-e-Khas, and Kila

Kohna with a protective wall, leading to the construction of numerous sarais and hammams.

The fort comprised various facilities such as arsenals, storage rooms for grains, and magazines, along with a palace situated in the citadel. Within the old fort, notable structures included the mausoleum of Nawab Faiz Mohammad Khan, a prison, and the ancient palace of Raja Kesari Singh, all of which were impressive edifices. Additionally, there were numerous impressive stone staircases leading down to the lake, skillfully crafted by Hindu residents of the city.[52]

Later on, Chhote Khan, Dewan of Nawab Hayat Mohammad, was buried within the fort after his death in 1795 CE at the age of 40. Amir Mohammad Khan succeeded Chhote Khan but was characterised as a weak yet tyrannical individual. He was eventually dismissed by the Nawab and had to retreat to Fatehgarh, from where he fired upon the city, causing damage to the fort and state subjects. However, he was forced to vacate the fort and sought refuge in Nagpur. Under the reign of Sikandar Jahan Begum and Shahjehan Begum, Fatehgarh underwent meticulous reconstruction, emphasising preservation and progress for which they received appreciation from British Officers.[53] A marble memorial dedicated to the martyrs of World War I, positioned on the left side of the gate of Fatehgarh Fort bears the inscription: *"Bhopal State... From this region, 994 individuals served in the great war of 1914-1919. Among them, 36 made the ultimate sacrifice."* [54]

In addition to fortifying the city, Nawab Dost Mohammad constructed several gates around the boundaries of the city of Bhopal. All of these gates emerged during a period of unrest and feudal wars. These gates served as both enclosures and protective barriers. A stone wall with six major gates was constructed: Peer Gate, Jumerati Gate, Itwara Gate, Budhwara Gate, Mangalwara Gate and Ginnauri Gate. However, except for Jumerati Gate, all the other gates are demolished now.

The architectural style of Gateways exemplified the Indo-Afghan style. The Afghan ruler introduced several innovative elements to the building style, including arches, beams, Mughal arches, massive gateways, extensive mouldings, decorative motifs, and jharokhas, which are characteristic of Islamic architecture. The jharokhas of the gate are decorated with buds and flower motifs and the elaborate ornamentation on the balcony balustrade.

Constructed in the 18th century CE, the Jumerati Gate was built subsequent to the construction of Fatehgarh Fort between 1720 to 1726 CE. Its purpose was to safeguard the fort and provide protection to the public. Located in the old city of Bhopal, it holds historical significance and is associated with the Jumerati Bazar. Having stood for centuries, Jumerati Gate has endured wars, weather, and riots. Over time, this area has been encroached upon by illegal shop owners, leading to various issues. Many of the shops surrounding the gate have been in existence for more than four generations.

However, the lack of proper maintenance has resulted in cracks and structural weakening of the gate. Additionally, the visual pollution caused by electric wires and water pipelines, as well as the environmental deterioration caused by moss formation and vegetative growth, have further contributed to its deterioration.

The gate was originally constructed using coursed rubble masonry with lime mortar and was covered with stucco. Over time, additional elements were incorporated into the conservation process.[55]

The fort of Fatehgarh houses a small mosque called the "Dhai Seedi Ki Masjid" (Two and a Half Steps Mosque), believed to be the first mosque of the Bhopal State. Some historians dispute its origin, suggesting it might have been a lookout post converted into a mosque later.[56] The mosque is located adjacent to the Tomb of Sardar Dost Mohammad Khan on the top portion of Fatehgarh Fort's Bastion. It is considered the smallest mosque in Asia.[57] The monument has two and a half stairs leading to the prayer hall, giving it its unique name. The mosque was likely used by the fort's guards to perform namaz. Currently, the main entrance is abandoned, and the remains of the Fatehgarh fort can be seen from the mosque.[58]

The Tomb and Masjid of Sardar Dost Mohammad Khan are located within the fort of Fatehgarh, now part of the campus of Gandhi Medical College. The tomb holds historical significance as the final resting place of the Founder of Bhopal State. Constructed by his son Yar Mohammad Khan in 1742 CE after his death in 1740 CE, the tomb features a dome-shaped pavilion resting on pillars. The main tomb is based on eight pillars, open from all sides and has a dome on its top, adorned with a beautiful lattice wall of marble around the main tomb.

Tomb of Sardar Dost Mohammad Khan

The pillars are intricately designed, contributing to the overall architectural style. The lower railings showcase intricate jali work, while lotus medallions adorn both the interior and exterior of the structure. The tomb is enclosed by 12 feet high walls with minarets on all four corners and is a protected monument of Madhya Pradesh Archaeology Department. A stone carrying the name of Dost Mohammad reads his name and titles: *Khan-i-Moazzam Masnad-i-Ale Diler Jung Sirdar Dost Moham-Mad Khan*. Fateh Bibi, Dost Mohammad's wife, was also cremated here. Beside the tomb, the masjid of Sardar Dost Mohammad Khan has undergone extensive renovation, leaving very little of its original construction.

03

NAWAB

YAR MOHAMMAD KHAN (1728-1743 CE)

On the death of Dost Mohammad Khan, the nobles put Sultan Mohammad Khan, a boy of eight, on the *masnad*. Yar Mohammad, who was at Hyderabad when informed of this by the Nizam, replied, "The place of a father is sufficiently taken by the protecting shadow of Your Highness." The Nizam, pleased with these words, promised his support and, after presenting Yar Mohammad with the Mahi Maratib, drums, banners, and other insignia of royalty, sent him to Bhopal, accompanied by a considerable force. No opposition was, however, offered, and he quietly deposed Sultan Mohammad and assumed the reins of government.

In 1739 CE, the Nizam was defeated by Baji Rao near Bhopal.[59] About this time, Nadir Shah crossed the Indus, entering Delhi in February 1739 CE. This event dealt a final blow to the weakened control of the Mughal emperors, and the governors of provinces were left to act as they liked. Wazir Akil Mohammad Khan died at this juncture, being killed, as mentioned earlier in a riot during Holi. He was succeeded in 1742 CE by Bijai Ram, a Hindu who proved himself an able minister.

Yar Mohammad Khan never actually assumed the title of Nawab. Major Henley mentions that it was arranged that whenever Sultan Mohammad entered the *darbar,* Yar Mohammad should rise to receive him and allow him to sit on the *masnad* during his visit.[60] He made Islamnagar his chief place of residence and, following in his father's footsteps, directed his energies towards extending his dominions and soon acquired possession of Udaypur, Sewans, and Pathari. He also came into conflict with the Marathas on several occasions, with a severe encounter taking place on the banks of the Kolans River near the villages of Borband and Beta (23°15' N.; 77° 24' E).

After ruling for fifteen years, he died in AH 1155 (1742 CE) and was buried at Islamnagar.[61] He left five sons, Faiz Mohammad Khan, Hayat Mohammad Khan, Sayad Mohammad Khan, Hassan Mohammad Khan, Yasin Mohammad Khan, and four daughters.

The Battle of Bhopal, which took place from December 1737 CE to January 1738 CE, was a significant conflict between the Nizam of Hyderabad and the Marathas. Both parties sought to control the strategic region of Malwa, as it held importance for their ambitions in both the North and South of India.[62]

The Nizam, accompanied by his son and a sizable army, marched from Delhi to Malwa to confront the Marathas. Meanwhile, the Marathas, led by Baji Rao, gathered a large force and joined by other influential figures, proceeded towards Malwa. Yar Muhammad Khan, despite his fears, allied with the Nizam upon arriving in Bhopal.[63]

However, the Nizam's cautious approach allowed the Marathas

to surround his army, leading to skirmishes but no decisive outcome. The Nizam eventually sought peace negotiations, resulting in the Convention of Doraha on January 6, 1738 CE. Under this agreement, the Marathas gained sovereignty over territories between the Narmada and Chambal rivers. The Nizam promised to secure confirmation of the treaty from the Emperor and attempt to obtain funds for Baji Rao.

Following the battle, the Marathas turned against the states that had supported the Nizam, including Bhopal. Baji Rao entered into a three-year agreement with Yar Muhammad Khan, who agreed to make financial contributions to the Marathas. Bhopal's contribution for the current year was promptly collected. The outcome of the Battle of Bhopal significantly weakened the Nizam's power, establishing the Marathas as a dominant force in India.

Masjid Nawab Yar Mohammad Khan, situated in Shehr-e-Khas, was constructed by its eponymous builder. This mosque stands amidst residential areas and occupies a space of 9.6m×19m. The prayer hall is upheld by sturdy and intricately crafted stone pillars. The structure, made of sandstone, remains well-preserved but lacks protective measures. Presently, ownership of the mosque belongs to The Wakf Board of Bhopal, Madhya Pradesh.

After ruling for fifteen years, Nawab Yar Mohammad passed away in 1753 CE at his capital, Islamnagar. His final resting place is a tomb located near the Islam Nagar fort, which can still be observed, albeit in a poorly preserved state. The tomb was surrounded by a lush green garden where other tombs like Hayat Muhammad Khan's Tomb were also constructed.

This square-shaped tomb of Yar Mohammad Khan stands on a small brick plinth. The primary construction material used is brick. Above the pillared hall, there is a Bangla dome with one finial at the centre and four at the corners. The tomb has three arches that open from each of the four sides, featuring unique cusped arch and ogee arch designs. Above the arches, beautifully decorated niches can be seen. The tomb is a load-bearing structure that has been adorned with lime plaster on its walls, arches, and pillars.

Yar Mohammad Khan's wife, Mamola Bibi, was actively involved in the administration of Bhopal after her husband's death, too. Mamola

Bibi, as Malcom mentions her in his text, was an extraordinary princess who lived to the advanced age of 80 and who, for more than half a century, greatly influenced the councils of Bhopal. She seems to have come from Upper Hindustan, but there are no official records of this. She was never publicly married to Yar Mohammad Khan and had no children, but considered his children to be hers; hence, she was given the title of Maji Sahiba. From the account given of her conduct under the most trying circumstances, it seems difficult to say whether she was most remarkable for the humanity of her disposition or the excellence of her judgement. She was beloved and respected by all. Mamola Bibi actively contributed to the infrastructure development work other than administrative tasks. She was the de facto ruler of Bhopal for fifty years and died in 1792 CE.

The construction of three masjids is attributed to the Mamola Bibi. The first mosque built by her was Maszid Maji Sahiba, Retghat in around 1730 CE. The mosque is approached through a cusped arched opening in a formal gate topped with slender finials. The prayer hall is spanned by octagonal pillars on a square stone base, with stone brackets projecting on all sides. The brackets are similar to the brackets in the tomb of Dost Mohammad Khan. The construction used here is non-Islamic in style.[64]

Another masjid constructed under the patronage of Mamola Biwi was Maszid Maji Sahiba Kala in 1745 CE. Located near Gohar Mahal, the mosque has semi-circular arched openings topped with a crenellated parapet. A pavilion with Bengali-style roofing is located in the centre of the elevation. Four slender and long turrets mark the end of the mosque walls. A perforated arched opening in the parapet faces the lake. The mosque is also known as the Old Jama Masjid.[65]

Masjid Qudsia Begum was also constructed by Mamola Bibi, but as Qudsia Begum came into power, it was renamed after her. The wide and high semicircular arches of the high-roofed prayer hall of the mosque are supported on carved, tapering twin stone pillars. The vaulted roof of the mosque gives it a greater height and is marked by four minarets at the four corners. Niches, Taqchas, and grooves decorate the walls of the interiors. Large cusped arched openings divide the courtyard from the prayer hall. The dividing wall between the mosque and Gauhar mahal has 10th-century CE architectural fragments embedded in the wall. The mosque, as said earlier, resembles other mosques by Mamola Begum, and a corner of the mosque cuts into Gauhar Mahal, giving evidence that this would have stood before the palace was built.[66]

आप

04

NAWAB FAIZ MOHAMMAD KHAN (1744-1777 CE)

Faiz Mohammad succeeded as a boy of 11, but not without opposition, as a party in the state wished to put Sultan Mohammad on the *musnad* and actually proclaimed his succession at Bhopal, Faiz Mohammad being at Islamnagar. Bijai Ram, however, acted with great promptness. He at once moved out of Islamnagar with a force of 5,000 men, while the Governor of Chainpur Bari, by professing sympathy with the succession of Sultan Mohammad, had obtained admission to the Fatehgarh fort at Bhopal. He manned the walls with troops and seized the gates, forcing Sultan Mohammad to leave the place. Bijai Ram arrived at this juncture, and a fiercely contested fight took place near the *Idgah,* to the north-west of the fort. Sayad Mohammad Khan, who commanded Faiz Mohammad's forces, was killed, and a panic was beginning when Bijai Ram sent up his reserves and retrieved the day. Sultan Mohammad fled to Nawab Izzat Khan of Korwai and then to Rahatgarh, where the Governor opened the gates to him. Bijai Ram at once laid siege to the fort, but the Mamola Bibi, the widow of Yar Mohammad, wisely counselled a cessation of these family dissensions, and Rahatgarh and the surrounding district were made over to Sultan Mohammad in jagir on his undertaking to renounce all claims to the chiefship.

Faiz Mohammad was by nature a religious recluse who took no interest in the administration of his state, which he left entirely to the Mamola Sahiba and his minister. The fort of Raisen was seized about this time by the Nawab's troops, with the Imperial Governor Nawid Ali Khan Khwajasera being killed. Somewhat alarmed at the possible results of this attack on an imperial official, the Nawab wrote to Delhi, explaining that he suspected the Governor of wanting to become independent and had taken this step to prevent it. In reply, he was thanked, and a *farman* was granted, making over the fort formally to the Nawab. About 1745 CE, the Marathas entered Bhopal and obtained possession of the parganas of Ashta, Devipura, Doraha, Ichhawar, Bhilsa, Shujalpur, and Sehore.[67] The battle of Panipat (January 6, 1761 CE) freed the state for a time from all fears of further Marathi invasion, and peace reigned until the Nawab's death in 1777 CE.

Diwan Bijai Ram died in 1762 or 1763 CE and was succeeded by Ghisi Ram, who favoured Hindus, forbade the killing of kine (bovine animals), and oppressed the Pathan nobles in every way. At length, two Pathans murdered him. His successor, Gairat Khan, was poisoned by a courtesan after six years in office. Lala Kesri, a Kayasth, succeeded. He was an able administrator and managed the state for fourteen years. He was eventually murdered by a confederacy of Pathans led by the Nawab's younger brother, Yasin Mohammad Khan, in revenge for an intrigue carried on by Munna Lal, the Diwan's son with a Pathani woman.[68] Yasin Mohammad Khan then succeeded to the wazirship.

Nawab Faiz Mohammad Khan was also known as Awalia Nawab, and an Urs is held every year in his honour. Dargah Faiz Bahadur was constructed in 1777 CE and is located in close proximity to Kamlapati Mahal and Kamla Park. It is a square structure with a projection of the roof just above the original mazar located at the centre. A verandah runs on all four sides of the mazar. Of the four sides, three have three bays, of which the central bay is open. The remaining two bays on all three sides are adorned with jaali work in red sandstone. The stone pillars are embellished with carvings of grape vines, ghat pallav, lotus, and various other patterns. It has crenellations on the parapet. The structure is currently maintained by the Waqf Board.[69]

05

NAWAB HAYAT MOHAMMAD KHAN (1777-1807 CE)

On December 12, 1777 CE (11th Zikat, 1191 AH) Nawab Faiz Mohammad died of dropsy and was buried in the fort. He was a man of gigantic stature, being nearly seven feet tall, but of a gentle and retiring nature.

As Faiz Mohammad died childless, his brother Hayat Mohammad succeeded him and was seated on the *masnad* on 1 Muharram 1192 AH (30 January 1778 CE). His succession was not uncontested. The late chief's widow, known as Bahu Begum, wished to be vested with the executive power while Sharif Mohammad Khan, the son of Fazil Mohammad Khan, and the son of Yasin Mohammad Khan, who had died a few days after the Nawab, were all preparing to dispute the succession. The lady's mother, Mamola Bibi, the widow of Yar Mohammad Khan, with a view to ending these dissensions, went to the Bahu Begum and pointed out that the rule must vest in some one person and that a brother of the late chief must be chosen, and finally persuaded her to acquiesce in the appointment of Hayat Mohammad, who was to act as deputy to herself, the Bahu Begum, thus retaining the real executive power. Soon after the conclusion of the arrangement, however, Hayat Mohammad Khan assumed the title and powers of Nawab, discarding the arrangement entered into with the Bahu Begum.

The result of the chief's indifference regarding the administration was the arrangement noted by Malcolm: of the whole revenue of the state, at this time amounting to 20 lakhs, 5 lakhs were set aside as the privy purse of the chief, which he was at liberty to spend as he wished, while the remaining 15 lakhs were devoted to state purposes. It was during the administration of Faulad Khan that Colonel Goddard made his famous march from Bengal to Bombay, passing through Bhopal territory.

In 1776 CE, the Bombay Government made the Treaty of Purandar, a treaty highly injurious to the interests and reputation of the East India Company, which they repudiated almost as soon as it was signed by actually supporting the candidature of Raghunath Rao (Raghoba) to the Peshwaship.[70]

In 1778 CE, Hastings decided to support the Bombay Government by sending a force from Bengal. A force consisting of six battalions of Native infantry and one company of Native artillery, to which was added a regiment of cavalry and a body of Mughal horses, sent by the Nawab of Oudh, started on February 23rd, 1778 CE, from Kalpi under the command of Colonel Leslie.[71,72,73]

Leslie, instead of marching south at once, mixed himself up in the local quarrels of the Bundela chiefs, and it was determined to supersede him. He died, however, on October 3rd, 1778 CE, and Goddard took over the command, and, proceeding by Bhilsa, Khemlása, Bhopal, and Hoshangabad, they crossed the Narbada on December 2nd. Through

Bhopal territory, he was given all assistance. Every effort was made to render the Nawab hostile, but without success, and although his territories suffered severely at the hands of the Marathas, he remained faithful to his promises although he was under no treaty obligations towards the British—a spontaneous act of generosity which was never to be forgotten.

Faulid Khan not long after this quarrelled with the Mamola Sahiba and was murdered by a member of the chief's family, and Chhote Khan, the Brahman convert, succeeded him on the 15th Zikat, 1194 AH (13th November, 1780 CE), on the advice of Mamola Bibi.

The selection of Chhote Khan was an admirable one. He maintained friendly relations with the great Maratha chiefs and was a sympathetic though a strong ruler who would brook no interference with his authority. A story is told of how he set free 400 Pindaris, who had been taken prisoners during a raid under the Pindari leader Hirs Bhao, by giving each man a pagri and some money. The Pindaris, astonished at such clemency, never again entered Bhopal territory during this minister's lifetime.

The Bahu Begum, annoyed at the strength of Chote Khan's rule, which prevented her from exercising her usual interference, instigated Sharif Mohammad Khan, a son of Fazil Mohammad Khan and grandson of Dost Mohammad Khan, to rebel against the orders of one whom she considered a mere slave raised to power by the Nawab. Begum offered to supply money if he would act, and Sharif Mohammad Khan raised a force, assisted by a large body of Pindaris. The Begum, at the critical moment, however, declined to advance the sum, and Sharif Mohammad, too deeply committed to retire, was obliged to do his best unsupported. He placed his family in safety at Ashta, then held by the Marathas, and made an advance on Ginnorgarh, the kiladar Kuli Khan being well disposed towards him. Here he encountered the forces of the state and was defeated. He then withdrew and marched straight towards Bhopal. At the village of Phanda (23°14' N. and 77°16' E.), he met the forces sent against him by Chhote Khan on the 16th *Jamadi-ul-Awal* 1201 AH (7th March 1787 CE). A fierce fight followed. Gradually, the forces of Sharif Mohammad gave ground and finally broke and fled, leaving Sharif Mohammad, his six brothers, and a few adherents on the field. Drawing their swords, his small band made a desperate attempt to cut their way through the ranks of the enemy, but only one brother, Kamil Mohammad Khan, succeeded through the extraordinary speed of his horse.

After this, Chhote Khan seems to have entirely changed his tactics and commenced to harass the Pathans in every way, not apparently without reason, as many plots were on foot for removing the Nawab and raising some other member of the family to the *masnad*. At length, a coalition was formed, headed by Najat Mohammad Khan, a son of Yasin Mohammad Khan, the Nawab's brother, a man noted for his great bodily strength. He chose the feast of *Eid-ul-Fitr*, when the Nawab always paid his respects to the Mamola Bibi. Stationing Kull Khan outside with some Pathans, he entered the palace and, after the usual greetings, seated himself by the Nawab. Najat Mohammad gradually brought the conversation around to Chhote Khan and his treatment of Pathans and insinuated that it was wrong that a mere slave should thus be granted authority, urging his dismissal or permission for him, the speaker, to kill him and remove this disgrace from the Afghan race.

The Nawab was very angry and retorted that Chhote Khan was no slave but his own adopted son, whose conduct had always been excellent and free from any suspicion of treachery. On this Najat, Mohammad drew his dagger and attacked the Nawab. Luckily, the chobdar, Parasram, heard the noise and, rushing in, felled Najat Mohammad with a blow of his silver mace, and other officers coming up dispatched him. Chhote Khan, after this event, increased his severity, instituting a rigorous system of police in the city. He also removed most of the Pathans from places of trust. These measures, though they did not allay the feeling of discontent, restored order. Chhote Khan paid much attention to public works, his best-known constructions being Chota Talab and Pukhtapul, or the stone bridge, which holds up the waters of the lower lake.

The lady Mamola died in the year 1792 CE, and Malcolm thus refers to her: The history of this extraordinary princess, who lived to the advanced age of eighty and who for more than half a century greatly influenced, if she did not control, the councils of Bhopal, is very extraordinary. Her name was Mumullah. She came from upper Hindustan, but seems to have been of too obscure an origin to leave any exact record of her parents or place of birth. Though she was never publicly married to Nabob Yar Mahomed, she became the principal lady of his family. She had herself no children, but all those of Yar Mahomed she considered her own, and the title of Maji Sahiba, or lady mother, which was given her by them and all others, proves the respect in which she was held. From the account given of her conduct under the most trying circumstances, it seems difficult to say whether she was most remarkable for the humanity of her disposition or the excellence of her judgement. She was beloved and respected by all. Her memory is still cherished by the natives, both Hindu and Mahomedan, of Bhopal, and it is consoling to see, in the example of her life, that even amid scenes of violence and crime, goodness and virtue, when combined with spirit and sense, maintain that superiority which belongs alone to the higher qualities of our nature, and which without these cannot be permanently conferred by neither title nor station.

Chhote Khan did not long survive his patrons, dying the same year on 26 Jamadi-ul-Akhir 1209 AH (18th January 1795 CE) at 40 years of age and being buried in the Fatehgarh fort. Though professing Islam, Chhote Khan was, in appearance, disposition, and manners, a Hindu.

Chhote Khan was followed by his son, Amir Mohammad Khan, a weak but tyrannical man who was soon dismissed by the Nawab. On his dismissal, he shut himself up in the Fatehgarh fort and commenced to fire on the city. He was, however, forced to evacuate it, and with the help of Amir Khan, Pindari, retired to Nagpur, where he entered the service of Raghuji Bhonsla and persuaded him to attack the fort of Hoshangabad, then in Bhopal State, which was captured in the early part of 1210 AH (1795 CE).

A clerk, Himmat Ram, was then made minister. Chhote Khan's widow retired to Sironj, where she was given a pittance by the Pindari leader Amir Khan, while Amir Mohammad, her son, entered into his service and later into that of Ghafur Khan of Jaora, in which place his mother was still living in 1822 CE.

The affairs of Bhopal were now far from satisfactory, and dissension was rife, with Hayat Mohammad's favourite lady and a eunuch called Gul Khojah having entire command of the administration, even calling on Sindhia's general Lakwa Dada to seize the fort of Raisen. The finances, moreover, were in utter confusion, the state overrun by Pindaris and threatened with annihilation by the Marathas, when a saviour providentially arrived.

One morning in the year 1795 CE, a stranger appeared at the city gates, accompanied by a few attendants, who, on being stopped by the guards, declared himself the son of Sharif Mohammad Khan and desired an interview with the Nawab. He called himself Wazir Mohammad Khan. The Nawab received him with effusion and asked him how he had lived since his father's death in 1786 CE. Wazir replied that since the banishment of his family he had served under Hamir Singh, Rawat of Rajgarh (1776–90 CE), and afterwards at Hyderabad. On the dismissal of Raja Himmat Ram, which took place a few months later, the Nawab wished to make him minister. This step was, however, opposed by his son Ghaus Mohammad Khan and his mother Asmat Begum, who were afraid of their masterful cousin and dreaded the revenge that he might take for his father's death. On this day, Hayat gave in and sent for Murid Mohammad Khan, son of Sultan Mohammad Khan, then living at Rahatgarh.

Murid arrived escorted by 1,000 followers on the 12th of Zika, 1210 AH (20th May 1796 CE). Murid Mohammad encamped at his father's garden outside the city, and, embracing the trees planted by his ancestors, began to weep and lament, behaving, as the chronicler puts it, "like a Hindu usurer." In his interview with the Nawab and Asmat Begum, he ingratiated himself through fulsome flattery, while his conduct towards the great merchants, officials, and soldiers was deferential and most submissive. The suspicions of the Pathan nobles, however, were roused by conduct that, in their eyes, was disgraceful and derogatory, and they anxiously awaited the development of the new minister's real character. Murid refused, however, to accept office until Bhopal was freed of strangers and Amir Khan, Pindari, who had been made kiladar of Fatehgarh fort by Ghaus Mohammad, had to retire. He then attacked the late minister Himmat Ram, confining him and his nephew Khiali Ram, then Governor of Berasia, for six weeks until they paid a fine of Rs. 10,000[74] and fled for refuge to Durjan Sal Khichi at Sironj. The state was now overrun by Pindaris and robbers of every description, and it was necessary to raise money to pay troops to oppose them. To obtain funds, therefore, Murid commenced a system of house taxation. Having grown bold, he at length aimed still higher.

On the 11th Rajjab 1212 AH (30th December 1797 CE), he called on Asmat Begum on the pretence of obtaining pecuniary aid from her, but in the midst of the conversation, in which he addressed her as his aunt, he suddenly called in three accomplices, who rushed behind the pardah and murdered the Begum and her attendants. Murid Mohammad, to save himself, gave out that this was done at the suggestion of her son Ghaus Mohammad. The real motives of his conduct soon became apparent as he seized the entire amount of wealth she had amassed. He then entered on a general career of oppression, so that "the people used to pray with uncovered heads at midnight for deliverance from him."

The next objects of his design were Ghaus Mohammad and Wazir. To accomplish their ruin, he stopped at nothing. Wazir had been sent to drive some Pindaris from the southern districts, and Murid wrote secretly to Rahim Khan, the governor of Chainpur Bari, to capture and kill him. The letter was, however, intercepted, and instead Wazir attacked the governor and seized Ginnaurgarh.

Even the supine Nawab Hayat Mohammad now began to see through the plans of Murid and sent for Kuli Khan to rid him of his tyrannical minister, promising him the reversion of his office. Wazir Mohammad also marched up and joined Kuli Khan, and they advanced on Bhopal together, Kuli Khan halting at Chulah village and Wazir by the Pukhtapul. Murid, now thoroughly frightened, called on Bala Rao Inglia, then Sindhia's governor at Sironj, for assistance and even hoisted Sindhia's flag on the battlements of Fatehgarh. Bala Rao came up with 30,000 men and encamped near the Idgah but demanded the surrender of a fort in Bhopal territory before he would act. On this day, Murid promised to give up Islamnagar. Murid also handed over the fort of Fatehgarh to Amir Khan, the famous Pindari leader then in Maratha service, and enjoined him to watch Ghaus Mohammad, accompanied Bala Rao to Islamnagar. Here they met with an unexpected rebuff. Moti Begum, the sister of Hayat Mohammad, was living in the fort. She at once ordered the kiledar to refuse them admittance, exclaiming that she recognised no authority on the part of Murid Mohammad to dispose of state fortresses and would allow no stranger to enter. The Marathas were received with a heavy fire and retired, Murid taking over Raisen to the Marathi commander instead of Islamnagar. A month later, Bala Rao appeared before the city with 40,000 men and encamped at Govindpura.

The Nawab and Wazir Mohammad prepared to oppose them, and a fierce fight took place on the spot now occupied by the Aish Farhat, Dilkhusha, and Afza Bagh gardens. The subahdar was forced to retire to Sironj, taking Murid Khan with him. It is probable, however, that victory would in the end have lain with the superior numbers of the Marathas, but fortunately for the state, Sindhia's difficulties with Lakwa Dada obliged him to recall Bala Rao, and the danger was averted (1798 CE).[75]

Rao imprisoned Murid, who committed suicide by swallowing diamond dust. Bala Rao Inglia, however, had such a low opinion of this schemer that he believed that he was shaming death and refused to allow the body to be buried until he was certain of the fact that decomposition had set in. Murid Khan's memory is still detested, and for long after, it was the custom for any Bhopali visiting Sironj to strike his grave with his shoe five times. Wazir Mohammad was now promoted to the position of minister, from which Kull Khan retired in disgust to his estate at Ambapani.

Wazir's first step was to recover Raisen, which, after some show of resistance, was surrendered on payment of Rs. 30,000 (1798 CE). Wazir next bribed the Governor to hand over Hoshangabad fort. A force was, however, at once sent to affect its recovery by the Raja of Nagpur, and after some days of resistance, the Bhopal troops were obliged to retire to Ginnorgarh, and Sakharam Bapu, the Bhonsla's general, reoccupied it. To assist him in his objective, Wazir formed an alliance with the Pindari leaders Karim Khan and Chitu, the latter being granted Chhipaner as a place of residence. The lost districts of Ashta, Sehore, Doraha, and Ichhawar were soon after recovered, while contributions were levied from Shujalpur, Berasia, Bhilsa, and Seoni (22° 29 N.; 77°30 E.) south of the Narbada. The condition of the state at this time is well illustrated by the fact that the revenue collections only amounted to Rs. 50,000, and Wazir was, therefore, driven to obtain funds as best he could.

Ghaus Mohammad was now becoming frightened at the rapidly increasing power of Wazir, but he was unable to find anyone to take his place. At length, he induced his father to transfer the wazirship to Akbar Khan, who, however, proved quite incapable of carrying on the administration. Differences became acute and resulted in a fight at Bishan Khera (23° 2' N.; 77° 37' E.) between the adherents of Ghaus Mohammad and Wazir.

Ghaus Mohammad then called in Mohammad Shah Khan from Sironj and Karim Khan, Pindari, from Shujalpur to Islamnagar, and Wazir was forced to retire for a time, but he returned soon after when dissensions arose between Karim Khan and Shah Khan. Ghaus Mohammad then (1806 CE) appealed to Sindhia to rid him of Wazir, to whom he promised the fort of Islamnagar and 4 lakhs in cash, besides a yearly payment of Rs. 61,000. These terms were accepted, but Sindhia took no active steps. At this juncture, Hayat Mohammad died on 16th Ramzan 1223 AH (6th November 1808 CE) at the age of 73.

Under the rule of Hayat Mohammad, a few civil projects were undertaken by competent ministers, but only a handful of them remain intact today. The political turmoil during his reign potentially hindered the city's infrastructure development. Masjid Hussain Bakshi, located in the neighbourhood of Sheher-e-Kha, was constructed in the late 18th century, possibly during Hayat Mohammad Khan's reign. The entrance is accessed through a gateway with a pointed arch, directly opening onto the street. The boundary wall adjacent to the gateway features crenellations. The prayer hall on the opposite end displays circular arches and a double pointed arch. This mosque is well-preserved and its upkeep is overseen by Madhya Pradesh Wakf Board.[76]

The construction of Pul Pukhta in 1794 CE marked a significant expansion of Bhopal. It was a stone masonry dam, 275 metres long and 21 metres wide, spanning the Ban Ganga and Patra valleys. This dam created a small lake known as Chhota Talab, about one-tenth the size of Bada Talab, collecting water from several earlier wells. Chote Khan, the Dewan of Nawab Hayat Mohhamad Khan, commissioned this project. Chhota Talab covers an area of 3.25 square kilometres and overflows into Patra Nallah in a cascade. An aqueduct connects

Chhota Talab and Pul Pukhta

Chhota Talab to the lower lake, controlling the flow of water. Pul Pukhta, made of dressed sandstone, was originally built to create a cantonment area for the Afghan troops, which eventually became known as Jehangirabad in 1840 CE, during the reign of Jehangir Mohammad Khan. This bridge provided direct access to Jehangirabad from Banganga, narrowing the gap between the two areas.[77,78]

The Gangaurwali Baoli, located in the Kazi camp area, was constructed during the 18th century CE. It derives its name from the Gangaur festival, a traditional Hindu celebration where the Gangaur idol was immersed in this very Baoli. The steps leading to the well begin before the structure and extend until the end of the building. This symmetrical structure measures 70 feet x 30 feet and features a central pillared hall surrounded by rooms. Notably, the flat brick roof showcases intricate floral designs, which are a significant characteristic of this edifice. The upper floors gradually recede from the centre, creating terraces that face the central opening. Inside the central pillared hall, stone pillars with cusped arches are prominently placed. Unfortunately, the Baoli is currently in a severely deteriorated condition, and the steps have been covered to create a flat surface, which has been encroached upon by shops. Furthermore, the Baoli is devoid of water at present. The structure is privately owned and requires urgent attention and restoration.[79]

◇◇◇◇◇◇◇◇◇◇◇◇◇◇◇◇◇◇◇◇◇◇

NAWAB GHAUS MOHAMMAD KHAN (1807 CE)

Ghaus Mohammad succeeded his father on 4 Shawwal 1223 AH (23 November 1808 CE), but Wazir Mohammad was still the real ruler. Ghaus Mohammad, however, wished to take the power into his own hands, and an opportunity soon presented itself. Early in 1224 AH (1809 CE), Sadiq Ali, the General of the Nagpur chief, who had just seized Chainpur Bari, was invited by Ghaus Mohammad to advance on Bhopal itself and expel Wazir. Unable to prevent this, Wazir retired to Ginnorgarh. Sadiq Ali remained six weeks in Bhopal. He then returned to Nagpur, leaving his agents in the city, but in order to make his compact with the Nawab more certain, he insisted on Ghaus Mohammad sending his son, Muir Mohammad Khan, with him as a hostage. Wazir now suddenly returned from Ginnorgarh, and his assault on the town at daybreak drove the Marathas out of the town and the fort.

On meeting the Nawab, Wazir rebuked him in no measured terms, and the weak chief pleaded that he had been led astray by certain people whom he named. Wazir sent for these men and executed them on the spot, Lalji Mustapha and Lala Rupchand were torn asunder by elephants, and Bakshi Beni Lal and Munshi Suraj Mal were blown away by guns, while two Brahmans were forced to drink cow's blood. Wazir, fearing that this last act might rouse Sindhia's wrath, pacified that chief by undertaking to carry out the terms promised by Ghaus Muhammed, even sending his eldest son as security for the payment of the four lakhs of rupees still due. A year later, Wazir recovered the districts seized by Sadiq All and then joined Amir Khan Pindari in an attack on the Nagpur forces near Saugor. Amir Khan fled, but Wazir pushed the attack home successfully.

At this particular time, it seemed that Wazir Khan was successful in convincing Ghaus Mohammad to withdraw to Raisen, thereby making Wazir Khan the dominant leader in the state. Consequently, the reins of power effectively shifted to Wazir Khan's family branch.

NAWAB WAZIR MOHAMMAD KHAN (1807-1816 CE)

Wazir made an ineffectual attempt to form a treaty with the British in 1811 CE, sending his agent, Inayat Masih, to Mr. Jenkins, the resident at Nagpur. He was, however, informed that he had not only consorted with professed plunderers such as Amir Khan but that his country was at that moment one of their asylums. Sir Barry Close, who was then cooperating with the Raja of Nagpur, had indeed received discretionary orders as to attacking Bhopal.

Wazir, thereupon, sent an agent to Colonel Close, pointing out that he had been driven by reasons of self-preservation to join the Pindaris and urging the claims of the family who had so nobly supported Colonel Goddard in 1778 CE, while expressing his readiness to accede to any terms proposed. In 1812 CE, negotiations were opened by the British Government with Raghuji Bhonsla, the Nagpur chief. These overtures he rejected, and it then appeared that he had made a compact with Sindhia to attack Bhopal and dispossess Wazir Mohammad.

In March 1812 CE, Sindhia's General Jagu Bapu made an attack on Bhopal but without success, the ostensible reason for this action being a delay in the payment of money due. A certain sum was paid over, and Jagu Bapu retired during the monsoon.

When the cold weather arrived, he returned together with the Nagpur troops under Badiq All, the Nagpur Commander, and commenced combined operations for the destruction of the Bhopal State, which the Nagpur Raja and Sindhia had secretly determined on. The town was at once besieged, and but for the heroic defence made by Wazir, whose exertions during the four months it lasted were superhuman, it would have fallen to the enemy.[80]

Though the siege was at length relinquished, it was only for a time, as Sindhia, determined to humble the pride of Bhopal, in March 1813 CE dispatched Jean Baptiste Filose and Jaswant Rao Bhan with a fresh force. That the result of this attack would have proved fatal to the state is certain, as the Pindari allies of Wazir had been won over to the enemy while his resources were at their lowest ebb. Jean Baptiste and Jaswant Rao, however, fell out and fought between themselves near Sehore. This postponed hostilities, but the attack would have been ultimately delivered had it not been for political developments. Caused Sindhia to withdraw his army.

In October 1814 CE, Wazir sent agents to Mr. Metcalf at Delhi and Mr. Jenkins at Nagpur with proposals for an alliance. Metcalfe, however, finding that the Nawab's agent was not invested with full powers, arranged for a meeting to take place in Bundelkhand between a fully accredited agent and Mr. Wauchope, the agent there.

Mr. Wauchope addressed the Nawab, who was informed that an alliance would be concluded on the conditions that British troops were given free passage through Bhopal territory and supplies; that a fort was made over as a depot to be converted into a military station later on; that all connections with the Pindaris were broken off; and that he undertook to carry on no negotiations with other chiefs except through the British Government. Wazir demurred at the surrender of a fort but accepted the other conditions. Mr. Strachey, the resident at Gwalior, on being informed of this, somewhat prematurely, considered that the treaty was practically concluded and informed Sindhia. Sindhis objected on the basis that Bhopal was a dependency of Gwalior, a claim which the Resident refused to admit on the grounds of the strenuous efforts made by Wazir Mohammad against Maratha aggression and the fact that no Bhopal chief had ever, by treaty or otherwise, acknowledged Maratha supremacy. Sindhia, however, refused to recall his troops, but the Nagpur chief, who was informed at the same time, recalled Sadiq Ali.[81,82] At this juncture, Lord Hastings ordered out the Presidency armies in the Deccan, Gujarat, and Bombay. The Nawab at the same time let it be generally known that he was under British protection, and at the end of January 1815 CE, he wrote to Mr. Wauchope saying that he would send an agent to Bands to conclude a treaty after the Muharram.

Sindhia, deterred by these proceedings, seized the occasion of the quarrel between Jean-Baptiste Filose and Jaswant Rao Bhan to recall his army.

The Nawab's agent did not arrive in Banda till April 15th, 1815 CE. In the meantime, Wazir Mohammad, contrary to the proposed terms, had privately opened up negotiations with Jean Haptate Filose and Nagpur. The Governor General, annoyed at these proceedings, gave orders that his representative should be dismissed without being granted audience. This was done, and all negotiations were for the time broken off, though Wazir was informed that "no ill-will was harboured against him and that it was merely because his conduct had shown that he had not a proper sense of the value of the connection offered to him or of the spirit in which it ought to have been received that the British Government for the present withdrew from the discussion of it.[83]

Wazir, in fact, did not wish to do more than avail himself of the reputation of the British power to ensure his security, fearing to bind himself in any way that would interfere with his political independence and free action in increasing his dominions. Relieved from immediate anxiety, Wazir did not press his goal of obtaining a treaty with the same insistence, though he continued his friendly communications with British officers. He was, up to the very hour of his death, almost engaged in predatory warfare. Finally, he fell ill at Timari van (23°4' N.; 78° 48' E.) village but proceeded as far as Deori (23° 8' N.; 78° 44' E.), where he died on 16 *Rabi-ul-Akhir* 1231 AH (16 March 1816 CE). Shehzad Masih, son of Inayat Masih, had the corpse conveyed to Bhopal, where it lies in a mausoleum in a garden to the north of the town. Wazir was 51 when he died, having ruled Bhopal for nine years. Malcolm thus describes Wazir: This principality, from the hour he assumed the government until that of his death, was threatened with destruction. Such a man could alone have saved it. Though he was as remarkable for prowess and valour as the most desperate of the Afghan race, he was in his manners mild and pleasing, but his look and stature were alike commanding, and there was in his disposition a sternness that inspired awe. He later gave way to habits of dissipation, which were believed to have shortened his existence.[84] All acquainted with the vicissitudes of his life deeply regretted his death at the moment it occurred. He ought to have lived to see his patriotic efforts repaid, to witness the citizens of the country saved from ruin and ushered up in happiness and prosperity by the administration he had courted all his life and on which his hopes were pinned up to the very last moment. This fate was set aside for a son who he chose as his successor, raised, and who showed in every manner that he was worthy of his father.

NAWAB NAZAR MOHAMMAD KHAN (1816-1819 CE)

Wazir Mohammad left two sons, Amir Mohammad Khan and Nazar Mohammad Khan, the elder of whom was a slave to habits of indolence and excess that had enervated his mind and body. Wazir, therefore, chose his second son Nazar Mohammad Khan to succeed him, and he was raised to the position of chief, though the title of Nawab remained with Ghaus Mohammad, who, however, had long since retired from all active participation in state affairs.

On Friday, 22 *Rabi-ul-Akhir* 1233 AH (28 February 1818 CE), Nazar married Gohur Begum, better known as Qudsia Begum, the daughter of Ghaus Mohammad. Nazar Mohammad's first act was to complete a treaty with the British Government. In the beginning of 1819 CE, Shehzad Masih visited Mr. Jenkins, the Resident at Nagpur, on behalf of the Nawab, who agreed to accept all the terms offered to Wazir Mohammad in 1814 CE. The Nawab also wrote to Mr. Wauchope. The Governor General, however, declined to take any action at the time, though he assured the Nawab of his goodwill.[85]

Towards the end of 1817 CE, Lord Hastings received permission to act against the Pindaris, and negotiations were immediately opened with all the native chiefs in India.

The Resident at Nagpur was instructed to offer Nazar Mohammad the terms proposed in 1814 CE, with the arrangement of details being left to Sir Thomas Hislop and Sir John Malcolm. Nazar Mohammad accepted without hesitation and cooperated to his utmost, proving a most valuable ally.

When the war was over, he was most useful in negotiating terms with the Pindari leaders, Namdar Khan and others, who were given asylum in his territories under his guarantee as to their good behaviour.[86]

A treaty was concluded on 26th February 1818 CE and ratified on 8th March 1818 CE. The treaty contained a stipulation requiring the Darbar to assist the British administration with an auxiliary force of 600 horses and 400 AQ, the origin of the Bhopal Battalion.

Nazar Mohammad, in order to comply with this demand, cheerfully sold his ornaments and jewellery, realising the fifty-one lakhs with which he was able to raise and equip this force. In return for his services, the five parganas held formerly by the Vinchur chief and the fort of Islamnagar, then in Sindhia's hands, were restored to him. The results were of incalculable benefit to Bhopal.

Nazar Mohammad, who before the conclusion of this treaty was actually the possessor of only a few strongholds beyond the walls of which he scarcely dared to venture, now found himself the lord of a princely domain, while his revenues, which at the death of his father amounted to little more than a lakh of rupees, collected with the greatest difficulty, rose at a bound to nearly fifteen lakhs, with the prospect of becoming nearly double this amount.

Just when a brilliant future seemed to await the State of Nazar Mohammad, he was killed by the accidental discharge of a pistol. On the 22nd of Muharram, 1235 AH (11th of November, 1819 CE), he went to Islamnagar to hunt. While dandling his little daughter, Sikandar Begum, his young brother-in-law, Faujdar Mohammad, aged eight, drew a pistol from his brother's belt and, in playing with it, accidentally discharged it, the bullet passing through Nazar Mohammad's head.

"There was," says Sir John Malcolm, "but one sentiment, that of the deepest regret, and no one sought to take advantage of the accident to promote his own interests. At a consultation of the principal chiefs, it was resolved to continue to attend the widow and ministers of the deceased prince until the pleasure of the British Government was known as to his successor, and it is remarkable that not the slightest effort was made to influence the judgement of the British agent, a sufficient proof of the absence of all design or guilt on this unfortunate occasion.

Nazar Mohammad was only 28 years of age when he died after governing Bhopal for three years and five months, but he left a name such as is attained by few in the longest life. His appearance was noble, and his manners were those of a prince who knew the value of possessing the hearts of his subjects.[37]

Though out of deference to Ghaus Mohammad, with whom he always remained in terms of the closest intimacy, he had never assumed the title of Nawab, he was always so addressed by the British Government, which took no notice of a nominal chief who had long abandoned all interest in the affairs of his state.

Nazar Mohammad's death at such a time was an irreparable blow. He was a man of noble presence, superior mind, and strong personality, gallant and honourable, devoted to the service of his state, and one whose rule was unstained by a single act of tyranny.

BAOLI AND BARADARIS (BAGH UMRAO DULLAH)

During the reign of Nazar Mohammad in 1817 CE, the Baoli and Baradaris (at Bagh Umrao Dullah) were constructed. An inscription on the baradari near the Baoli credits Nazar Mohammad with the construction of the Baoli.

This octagonal structure consists of two stories and is partially submerged in water. The stepped well was likely connected to a fountain in the garden. The upper part of the structure is made of intricately carved flagstone slabs, featuring carved brackets and cusped arched openings.

Initially, there were several copper fountains in the vicinity, connected to the Baoli through copper pipes, although these may have been added at a later time. Two baradaris in the area, believed to have been built during the same period, have been modified and are currently used as residences.[87]

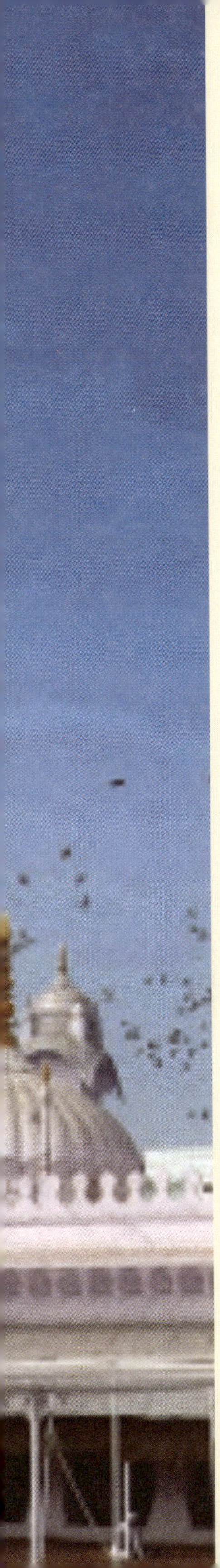

09

NAWAB

QUDSIA BEGUM (1819-1837 CE)

Qudsia Begum's reign began when she stood up in front of the congregation at her husband Nazar Mohammad's Soyem (a post-death ritual) and addressed the gathering by stating how the legacy of their family must be maintained, thus declaring her 15-month-old daughter Sikandar as the rightful heir. Her speech, coupled with the fact that she took off her veil before making it, was an act of agency that was unprecedented for Muslim women of that time. As Shaharyar M. Khan says in his account of the Begums of Bhopal, "Qudsia's address to the family is one of the most poignant moments in Bhopal's history. A girl not yet 20 brought up traditionally in Purdah had dared to take the congregation of elders, rival family contenders, and senior state officials by the scruff of their necks".

Qudsia Begum was appointed regent until her daughter was old enough, the assumption being that Sikandar would marry and her husband would become the Nawab of Bhopal. With the consent of the nobles of Bhopal and the British government, it was decided that Nazar Mohammad's nephew, Munir Mohammad Khan, should succeed under the regency of Qudsia Begum and eventually marry her daughter, Sikander Begum. Munir Mohammad's authority was opposed by Qudsia Begum. Mr. Meddocks, a political agent of the East India Company, interfered to solve the matter between the two. An arrangement was made in which Munir Mohammad consented to resign in favour of his brother Jehangir Mohammad Khan for a compensation of Rs. 40,000 a year. It is believed that Qudsia Begum, wanting to retain power in her hands, delayed the marriage of her daughter. Despite her mother's best efforts, Sikander Begum was married to Jehangir Mohammad Khan on 17th April 1835 CE. He continued to administer the state which caused differences between Qudsia Begum and the young Nawab Jehangir Mohammad Khan. With time, conflict arose between the Nawab and Sikander Begum as well.

Qudsia Begum took many clever steps to guarantee her position: she made deals with her rivals for power, approached a British agent to legitimise her status, and garnered support from religious authorities to combat the widely held belief by Muslims that women could not rule. The state Qazi (judge) and Mufti (jurisconsult) signed a document acknowledging women's right to political power.

She was the first woman in South Asia to successfully assert the right of Muslim women to legally be the rulers of a state. Being a devout Muslim herself, she showed that Islam does not exclude women from gaining political power. She commanded the army and would be at the forefront of battles.

One day, on the occasion of a feast, Nawab Jehangir Mohammad plotted to forcefully seize Qudsia Begum and Sikander Begum, but the Begums escaped safely to their palace and dispatched a military force to capture the Nawab. On the command of the British government, she retired from the administrative affairs of Bhopal with a grant of

Rs. 5 lakhs per annum. In 1877 CE, she was decorated with the Order of the Imperial Cross. She passed away after four years at the age of eighty-two and bequeathed her personal property to her granddaughter, ShahJehan.

No major construction took place due to repeated attacks on the city until about 1819 CE, when an alliance with the British government finally materialised. This treaty ensured the city against invasion, and economic prosperity returned to the city with various socio-political infrastructures coming up in the city.

Several construction projects took place during the glorious reign of Qudsia Begum. Wazir Bagh, Noor Bagh, Nazar Bagh, and Bagh-e-Kalan combine to form Bada Bagh, which covers a large area of around 32 acres. This was set up by Nawab Qudsia Begum in 1819 CE in memory of Nawab Wazir Mohammad Khan. The graves of the members of the ruling family of Bhopal can be found here. The Baoli at Bada Bagh is a three-story deep octagonal structure with a wide flight of steps leading to the water. The ornamental structures that surround the well are colonnades with cusp arches and slender stone pillars.[88]

Aish Bagh and the Baoli were constructed by Nawab Qudsia

Bada Bagh Baoli

Begum in the 1820s CE. It contained many large trees, a small mosque, and a very fine Baoli. The rose plants were well decorated and surpassed even the famous Lal Bagh of Bangalore. The Baoli is a cool, ventilated structure where a central staircase leads to the water, which is at a depth of 6 m.

The Baoli was surrounded by four sturdy brick walls and featured numerous brick wells, fruit trees, and fragrant roses. Adjacent to it, there was a grand masonry structure along with a small mosque and multiple summer houses, adding to its overall charm.[89]

She was also responsible for the "Aish Bagh" (Garden of Delight), a beautiful garden in the oriental style with a large pleasure house, a small mosque, and some other buildings in it. This garden was given to Nasrullah Khan by her mother Sultan Jahan Begum.[90]

Gauhar Mahal, one among the oldest palaces in Bhopal, holds significance as one of the important residences of the Nawabs from the princely state. The exact date of its construction is uncertain, but it is believed to have been built during the reign of Nawab Nazar Mohammad Khan (1816-19 CE) or possibly earlier. The palace was named Gauhar Mahal in honour of Qudsia Begum (also known as

Gauhar Mahal

Gauhar Begum), the wife of Nawab Nazar Mohammad Khan.

According to the book *Hayat-e-Sikandari,* Sikandari Jehan Begum was born in 1818 CE in a room called Balai Manzil within this palace. This suggests that at least a portion of the palace existed even before Qudsia Begum's reign (1819-1837 CE). The sprawling complex consisted of various buildings, including Nazar Mahal, Bibi Ki Masjid, Gauhar Masjid, Kudsia Bagh, Diwan-e-Aam (for the general public), a rectangular large courtyard known as Diwan-e-Khas (for the elite), and a residential complex. Additionally, there was a triangular courtyard that housed the offices.

The architectural style of the palace is a fusion of Mughal, Rajput, and local influences. The Mughal influence can be seen in the multicoloured arches on the pillars of Diwan-e-Khas and the flower motifs on the gate. The blend of Mughal and Rajput styles is evident in the balcony brackets on the upper floor and the courtyard. The wooden doorways in the interior showcase beautiful carvings that combine elements of Gujarat, Rajasthan, and Malwa styles. Carved windows, ornate door frames, balconies, lotus flowers, and various arches and pillars add to the grandeur of the architecture.

The construction materials used included plaster's wood, lakhauri (brick), lime, sarsi (a type of mortar), and gum. After the construction of Shaukat Mahal, Hawa Mahal, and Moti Mahal, Gauhar Mahal ceased to be the residence of the Nawab family and was repurposed as the princely offices. With the construction of Gauhar Mahal, the administrative nucleus of the city shifted. Oriented southwest, the palace contained both private and public spaces. Over time, the building underwent changes and additions to accommodate the needs of various government departments, such as the Muhafiz Khana (Records Office), agriculture, manufacturing, and land records. The rooms in one section of the building were also used for the District Head Office of Bhopal and Raisen districts.[91]

Masjid Nur, built in the 1820s CE, stands in close proximity to Jami Masjid in Shehr-e-Khas. One of its notable features is the crown adorning the parapet above the entrance. The mosque showcases impressive architectural elements, including intricately carved stone pillars, cusped arches, and niches. It is speculated that the mosque may have been named after Nur Mohammad Khan, the father of Dost Mohammad Khan.[92]

Constructed with a combination of bricks and stones held together by lime mortar, the mosque is a registered Waqf property and remains in good condition, though lacking government protection.

The oldest church of Bhopal, St Francis of Assisi Cathedral was previously called "The Roman Catholic Church" and belonged to the Bourbon family of France. It was built during Begum Qudsia's reign by the widow of Shahjad Masih, son of Salvador Balthazar, under the supervision of Father Bernard Pistoia. The church is located in the Jehangirabad area.

The church has large circular windows and arches, supported on circular pillars of double height. Coloured glass is used in the windows. It is 30m x 60m, rectangular in shape and faces north. The facia is new but the original dome and spire can still be seen behind the facade. It is in private ownership now and is in fair state of conservation.[93]

Located in ShahJehanabad, in close proximity to the Taj Mahal Palace and Marghatiya Mahaveer Mandir, Lal Darwaja was constructed during the reign of Qudsia Begum in around 1830 CE and later became a part of the larger Taj Mahal Palace complex. It served as the entrance gate to Bada Bagh, the royal graveyard. However, the graveyard no longer exists, and the pathway has shifted, now running alongside the gate. It follows a typical Islamic-style architectural design and is constructed on a square platform. It consisted of guard rooms at both sides that have been closed now. The gateway itself is a two-story structure, situated adjacent to the main road at present.[94,95]

The Jama Masjid of Bhopal, situated amidst the planned design of *Shehr-e-Khas,* is a remarkable architectural masterpiece built by Nawab Qudsia Begum. Construction began in 1248 AH (1832 CE) and was completed in 1273 AH (1857 CE) at a cost of 565000 rupees, 2 annas and 9 pies. It took about twenty-five years to complete and is one of the finest mosques in the heart of the city.[96]

Made of red sandstones, the mosque's architecture is based on the four-garden system found in Delhi's Jama Masjid.[97] The impressive structure boasts entrances from three directions and a spacious courtyard. A significant feature of the Jama Masjid is its three bulbous domes, which are visible from a distance, along with a sequence of white plastered alabaster arches that lavishly decorate its interior. The qibla wall is adorned with beautifully crafted meharabs featuring well-known ogee curves. The most renowned feature of the mosque is its two imposing minarets, a unique design in India, crowned with gold spears. The mosque's airy open courtyard, with covered passages on the north and south, showcases impressive Islamic structural design. The sanctuary houses three aisles with a central access strip running from north to south. The wings on both sides of the nave have four-sided barrel-vaulted hallways and square halls at the extreme end. Round its basement there were a number of shops whose rent form part of the endowment of the mosque.[98] The inscription on the northern gate of the Jama Masjid translates to the following: "The construction of the Jama Masjid began in the early part of the year 1248 AH (1832 CE) according to the Fasli calendar. It was initiated by the generous and virtuous Nawab Gauhar Begum Saheba, daughter of Nawab Gous Mohammad Khan and wife of the late Nawab NaziruddaulahNazae Mohammad Khan Bahadur. The construction was completed at the end of the year 1273 AH (1857 CE). Eminent architects contributed to its strength and beauty, and through the careful management of honest individuals, it incurred a cost of five hundred and sixty-five thousand rupees, two annas, and nine pies. This inscription was written by Mohammad Abbas Shirwani." Round its basement there were a number of shops whose rent form part of the endowment of the mosque.[99]

A legend among locals speaks of the vast number of pigeons residing in and around the mosque, believed to be descendants of a pair brought from Mecca-Madina.

Interestingly, the mosque was built on the site of an old Hindu temple called the Sabha Mandal, constructed in 1151 CE by Rani Shalmali, wife of Paramara King Udayaditya.[100]

Situated in Shehr Khas, the temple was constructed by Qudsia Begum to enshrine the idols discovered during the construction of Jama Masjid at the site. According to the trust members, the temple's construction involved utilising the remains of Sabha Mandal. Notably, the temple boasts intricately carved pillars with Keechaka capitals dating back to approximately the thirteenth century. Covering an area of 28 m x 36 m, the temple is made of sandstone and is reasonably well-preserved. It is currently owned by the Shri Digamber Jain Panchayat Committee Trust.[101]

This is the second temple constructed by Qudsia Begum to accommodate both sects of the Jain community. Located in the bustling Chowk Bazar, the double-story structure features a large entrance gateway resembling the residences in the area. The three-dome shikhara is not visible from the exterior as it does not project beyond the building's facade. Such temples, known as Haveli Temples, emerged during the Islamic rule, with the garbhagriha housed within the haveli.[102]

Access to the temple is through an entrance that leads to a double-height hall surrounded by a pillared portico. The garbhagriha faces the entrance across the hall. Managed by the Shwetamber Jain Murti Pujak Trust, the temple is well-maintained and preserved in good condition.

Located within the Iqbal Maidan Complex, Masjid Toshakhana is situated alongside Sadar Manzil and Gauhar Mahal, making it a part of a historically significant area. The mosque bears an important inscription by Qudsia Begum, indicating its construction in 1267 Hijri, which corresponds to approximately 1850 CE. Qudsia Begum commissioned the mosque during the reign of Sikander Begum, showcasing her patronage towards this architectural gem.[103]

The mosque has a modest size and features circular and ogee

Jama Masjid

arches, giving it a unique architectural character. A corrugated sheet projects into the courtyard, supported by delicate wooden pillars. Constructed using bricks and plastered with lime, the mosque is covered with stone slabs supported by timber rafters for its roof. The property is owned by the waqf board and has been well-preserved over the years, maintaining its historical and architectural significance.

Pushpa Nagar Baoli takes the form of a rectangular structure featuring expansive steps that descend to a depth of 10 metres, leading to a tank. This edifice was probably constructed during the reign of Qudsia Begum, alongside several other Baghs that were built in the same era. The steps are adorned with chambers on either side. Additionally, ornate arches and embellished openings showcase intricate mouldings and exquisite stucco work contributing to the aesthetic appeal of the Baoli. The unprotected monument is currently in a bad state of preservation.[104]

Raja Khushwant Rai Saxena was the first Wazir e Ala (Prime Minister) of Bhopal State. A memorial structure, known as the chhatri, was built in his honour. The chhatri is an octagonal-shaped monument constructed of sandstone and stands on a 15m x 15m high platform. Accessible from the north via a flight of steps, the octagonal structure features eight arched gateways on both the outside and inside. However, the central roof of the chhatri is now missing.

The platform on which the chhatri stands is adorned with decorative elements. Adjacent to the chhatri, there is a Baoli (stepwell) also named after Raja Khushwant Rai Saxena. Both the chhatri and the Baoli were built as a memorial for the Wazir. The chhatri is also a resting place for Raja Khushwant Rai Saxena's wife, Rani Amaan Bai.

Raja Khushwant Rai Saxena served as a minister during the reign of Nazar Mohammad and then Qudsia Begum in Bhopal State. As a prominent figure in the state's history, his memorial, the chhatri, and the Baoli are now protected monuments under the State Archaeology Department.[105]

◇◇◇◇◇◇◇◇◇◇◇◇◇◇◇◇◇◇◇◇◇◇

10

NAWAB JEHANGIR MOHAMMAD KHAN (1837-1844 CE)

On 1st *Ramzan* 1253 AH (30th November 1837 CE), Nawab Jehangir was duly invested with powers. Relations between the Nawab and his Begum remained strained, however, and she and her mother retired to Islamnagar, where a daughter was born to Sikandar Begum on 6th *Jamadi-ul-Awal* 1254 AH (29th July 1838 CE) and was named ShahJehan Begum. The Nawab took considerable interest in his state and initiated many improvements, one of which was the removal of the army from the heart of the town to the Jehangirabad quarters across the lake. He was also fond of literary studies and was a great patron of men of learning. He died on 28th Zikit 1260 (9th December 1844 CE) at 27 years of age and was buried in Noor Bagh.

The Palace of Jehangir Mohammad Khan, also known as Jehangirabad Kothi, was constructed as a private residence during Khan's reign (1837-44 CE). Located in the Jehangirabad area, which served as a new suburb and cantonment for the Bhopal army under Khan's establishment, the palace now serves as the police headquarters. In 1860 CE, a French traveller named Louis Rousselet stayed at this palace during his visit to Bhopal.

Originally called Moti Bungalow, the palace is a single-story structure that used to be surrounded by a garden known as Noor Bagh. This garden was watered by an extensive aqueduct, stretching for two and a half kilometres, which carried water from the lower lake to the garden. Remnants of an aqueduct can be observed on the southeast bank of Chhota Talab. Water was raised to a height of about 15 metres using the Persian technique called "Chawars," utilising leather bags and animal power, such as bulls, to lift water from wells. This water was then conveyed through channels on top of a gradually sloping arched wall and travelled a distance of 1.75 kilometres, eventually flowing into a pond. The pond served Noor Bagh and fulfilled the water needs of the Afghan troops stationed in the area.[106] The wheel itself is no longer present.

NAWAB SIKANDAR JAHAN BEGUM (1844-1868 CE)

1ST PERIOD

Nawab Nazar Mohammad Khan left one child, an infant daughter, Sikandar Begum. It was arranged with the consent of the Bhopal nobles and the sanction of the British Government that Nazar Mohammad's nephew, Munir Mohammad Khan, the son of his elder brother Amir Mohammad Khan, should succeed under the regency of

Gohur Begum, better known as Qudsia Begum, and should eventually marry Sikandar Begum, thus securing the rule in Wazir's branch. To this arrangement, neither Ghaus Mohammad nor any member of his immediate family raised any objections.

In 1827 CE, however, Munir Mohammad attempted to assert his authority but was opposed by Qudsia Begum. Several encounters took place between adherents of either party. Finally, Mr. Maddocks, the political agent, interfered, and an arrangement was reached by which Munir Mohammad consented to resign in favour of his younger brother Jehangir Mohammad Khan, receiving as compensation a jágir of 40,000 rupees a year. At this juncture, the favourite minister of the late chief, Hakeem Shehzad Masih (Balthazar Bourbon), who was the chief director of affairs and whose advice had proved invaluable, died on the 24th *Jamidi-ul-Akhir* 1244 AH (1st January 1829 CE). Qudsia Begum was anxious to retain the power in her own hands for as long as possible. With this view, she delayed, on one pretext or another, the marriage of her daughter with the Nawab. In 1833 CE, however, the Nawab visited Lord W. Bentinck at Saugor, and while there, he preferred a request that he might be granted administrative powers. Although the Viceroy was not prepared to support this request, he sent a message through the Political Agent urging Qudsia Begum to celebrate the wedding with her daughter. Qudsia Begum was annoyed at the pressure thus put upon her, but finally, on 18th Zulhijjah 1250 AH (17th April 1835 CE), the wedding was solemnised. Qudsia Begum, however, continued to administer the state, which caused differences to arise between her and the Nawab.

Dissensions also arose between the Nawab and Sikandar Begum. Finally, in 1837 CE, matters reached a crisis. On the occasion of the feast of Abdul Kadir Ghilániheld on the 11th *Rabi-ul-Akhir* 1252 AH (26th July 1836 CE), information was received that a plot had been concocted by the Nawab to seize the two Begums on their return from the feast. The Begums contrived to escape in safety to the palace, while a force was at once sent to confine the Nawab within his own residence.

On the 24th *Zulhijjah* (1st April 1837 CE), however, the Nawab managed to escape to Sehore, where he borrowed money and raised a force with which he seized the districts of Doraha, Devipura, and Jharkhera, and soon after obtained Ashta fort, to which the kiladar admitted him.

A force was at once sent against Ashta under the minister Raja Khushwakt Rai, who was accompanied by Lala Baijnath as a representative on behalf of the political agent. A fight took place on the Punbas River near the village of Kotra, in which some 300 people were killed and wounded. The Nawab was forced to retire into the fort, which was besieged. The besiegers, however, suffered severely from the rain and especially from a severe flood on the Punbas on 23rd August 1837 CE, which swamped their own camp. Matters were becoming serious when, at length, the Political Agent, Launcelot Wilkinson, acting under orders from the Governor General, sent Munshi Beni Prasad to Ashta to request Raja Khushwakt Rai to withdraw his troops. He accordingly returned to Bhopal on September 10th, 1837 CE.

The Nawab then went to Sehore. A few days later, the political agent arrived in Bhopal with the Bhopal contingent and encamped at Wazir's Garden. He informed Begum that the Governor General's instructions were that she should take over the administration in accordance with the original agreement and that suitable allowances would be made for her.

The Begum then consented to retire, receiving a life grant of five lakhs (Bhopal coins) per annum. In 1877 CE, on the occasion of the Imperial Assemblage at Delhi, she was decorated with the order of the Imperial Cross. She died in 1881 CE at the age of 82, leaving personal property worth five lakhs, which she bequeathed to her grand-daughter ShahJehan.

2ND PERIOD

Nawab Jehangir Mohammad Khan died on 28th Zikit 1260 (9th December 1844 CE), at the age of 27. He left a will in which he desired that his illegitimate son Dastgir be recognised as his successor and that his daughter ShahJehan by Sikandar Begum be married to a descendant of Wazir Mohammad Khan of pure blood.

The will in favour of Dastgir was set aside by the government, and several plots to place him in power were frustrated. The British Government recognised the succession of ShahJehan in the same manner as, on the death of Nazar Mohammad Khan, it had admitted the claims of Sikandar Begum, and it was decided that the future husband of ShahJehan, who was to be selected from the Bhopal family with a view to the amalgamation of the two branches descended from Ghaus Mohammad Khan and Wazir Mohammad Khan, should be chief of Bhopal. In the meantime, Faujdar Mohammad Khan, brother of Qudsia Begum, was to act as minister, receiving cooperation from Sikandar Begum. On 3rd *Rabi- ul-Akhir* 1261 (11th April 1845 CE), ShahJehan Begum, then 7 years of age, arrived in Bhopal and was proclaimed chief of the state, the regency being entrusted to her mother, Sikandar Begum, with Mian Faujdar Mohammad Khan, the youngest son of Nawab Ghaus Mohammad Khan, as minister.

This arrangement was not a success, as Sikandar Begum acted independently of the minister, and the dual rule soon produced an impasse. In 1846 CE, a disturbance was caused by Amir Mohammad Khan, paternal grandfather of ShahJehan, who raised a following and seized Kaliakheri fort. He was, however, dislodged by a detachment of the Bhopal Contingent from Sehore and confined in Asirgarh Fort, where he died in 1851 CE. The political agent then reported that there was no hope of peace until the dual rule was broken up. Mian Faujdar Mohammad had to resign, and the administration was left to Sikandar Begum until her daughter came of age. Sikandar Begum was an admirable administrator and effected many salutary reforms, including the abolition of the farming of revenues and trade monopolies, the reorganisation of the army, police, and mints, and the liquidation of the state debts. She toured regularly in her districts and examined the condition of her cultivators.

An interesting view of the Begum is given by Major Charters Macpherson, the Political Agent, who, writing in 1854 CE, notes that all three Begums were out of pardah: Qudsia, Sikandar, and ShahJehan, the last of whom was then just 16:

"The grandmother and mother ride, spear, and shoot grandly or have been used to do so.... The Regent is a wonderful woman in the way of government.... She talks exactly in her way like the fastest European woman you may happen to know, for example, mixing politics with her personality.... happened to say somewhat emphatically that everything depended on the way a system was worked, on the Umal that everything in fact was Umal, and wished you had seen how she turned to her two ministers (Jamiluddin Khan and Lala Kishan Ram) sitting dumb some way off and cried, 'Gentlemen, do you hear, that's for

everything... She shows a fine Elizabethan taste in the choice of her officers of state.[107]

On the 11th Zikat 1271 AH (26th July 1855 CE), the marriage of ShahJehan Begum was celebrated with Bakshi Baki Mohammad Khan, the Commander-in-Chief of the State Army. He was recognised as a Nawab consort and was granted the title of Nawab-Nazir-ud-daula Umrao Dula Bahadur and a personal salute of 17 guns. Sikandar Begum was to continue as Regent until her daughter was 21. In AH 1273 (1857 CE), came the Mutiny. Throughout this period, no chief in the length and breadth of India proved a stauncher ally than Sikandar Begum.

As in 1778 CE, again at this crisis, the Bhopal State proved itself a true friend of the British Government. By her most strenuous exertions, she kept the peace throughout her own territories, although the Maulvis in Bhopal city were preaching the jihad and she was being personally threatened by her troops. Colonel Durand, the Agent to the Governor General, retreating from Indore, was given temporary asylum at Sehore and then escorted to Hoshangabad, and fugitives from all sides were given assistance and placed in safety. But Sikandar Begum's efforts did not stop here. She gave all the assistance in her power to British troops outside her dominions, sending supplies of grain and forage as far north as Kalpi and detachments to keep the peace in Saugor and Bundelkhand. Fazil Mohammad Khan and Adil Mohammad Khan, the jagirdars of Ambapani, who rebelled, were at once attacked and their estates confiscated, while the refractory Kilidar of Rahatgarh, who refused to admit the British, was seized and impaled. When the Bhopal contingent troops at Sehore mutinied, she sent a force to overawe them and restore peace, also taking charge of the government treasury.[108]

On the restoration of order, Sikandar Begum urged her claims to be regarded not as Regent but as the ruling chief of Bhopal, on the strength of her services during the Mutiny and also on the grounds that the recognition of her late husband Jehangir as Nawab was technically wrong, in the same way that her daughter ShahJehan was in fact the legitimate ruler. ShahJehan Begum who had come of age on July 20th, 1858 CE, and was entitled to be invested with administrative powers, herself came forward and assented to the investiture of her mother as chief, waiving all claims to the *masnad* during her lifetime. The British Government acceded to this, and on 9th *Shawal* 1276 (3rd March 1860 CE), Sikandar Begum was formally installed as chief at Bhopal by the agent to the Governor General, Mr. Hamilton.

On 7th January 1861 CE Sikandar Begum visited the Viceroy at Jabalpur. Here in open *darbar* the Begum was presented with a *sanad* conferring on her the Berasia pargana confiscated from the Dhar State. The Viceroy, Lord Canning, addressed her with these words:

"Sikandar Begum! Your Highness is very welcome at this darbar. I have long desired to thank you for the services that you have rendered to the Queen's Government. Your Highness is the ruler of a state that is conspicuous in history for never having been in arms against the British power, and lately, when that state was beset and threatened by our enemies, you, a woman, guided its affairs with a courage, an ability, and a success that would have done honour to any statesman or soldier......... Such services must not go unrewarded.

I now place in your hands the grant of sovereignty of the district of Berasia. This district was formerly a dependency of the State of Dhar, but Dhar has by rebellion forfeited all claim to it; and it is now given in perpetuity to Bhopal for a memorial of loyalty, under your wise and brave guidance in a time of trial............"

In November of the same year Sikandar Begum was invested with the Grand Commander of the Star of India (GCSI), an order of chivalry established by Queen Victoria, at Allahabad. In the same year, she toured through India, visiting the cities of Benares, Jaunpur, Lucknow, Cawnpore, Agra, Delhi, Jaipur, Ajmer, Nimach, and Agar. In 1862 CE, Sikandar Begum received the *sanad* of adoption. In 1863 CE, she again visited the Viceroy at Agra, stopping on the way at Gwalior, where she was entertained by Sindhia. In the next year, she started on a pilgrimage to Mecca, accompanied by Qudsia Begum and Mian Faujdar Mohammad Khan, the first Mohammadan ruling chief to visit the holy shrine. She returned on 10th June 1864 CE.

In 1866 CE, she for the third time visited the Viceroy at Agra, and afterwards went to Bharatpur, Muttra, Dholpur, and Datia. She fell ill soon after her return and died on 30th October 1868 CE, at 51 years of age. She was buried in the Farhat Afza garden, which she had laid out.

Moti Mahal, located in Sadar Manzil, is a residential palace

Sadar Manzil

constructed in 1847 CE. by Nawab Sikandar Jahan Begum. It has three wings, creating two unequal-sized courtyards. The palace is symmetrically designed, with a three-story entrance at its centre, adorned with decorative elements like a semi-circular arch, jharokha projection, and a crown on the parapet. The facade features pilasters, false bangladar roof in stucco work, and a row of arches and pillars, resembling a sports pavilion.

The palace complex includes royal quarters, durbar hall, administrative areas, stores, and archives. The fresco paintings on the walls display golden, blue, brown, green, and silver colours. Built with brick and lime mortar, the palace was restored in the 1990s CE by the Environment and Planning Coordination Organization (EPCO), a government undertaking. However, the palace remains unprotected to date and extensively used for film shooting.[109]

Moti Mahal Gate, a two-storey structure with a width of six metres, was built during the reign of Sikandar Jahan Begum. Its purpose was to provide access to Sadar Manjil, the official courthouse of Bhopal. The gate features staircases on both sides, leading up to the roof, connecting Shaukat Mahal and Moti Mahal. The architectural style of the gate bears resemblance to that of Shaukat Mahal, which exhibits influences from French architecture. A structure called Muhafiz Khana, located between Moti Masjid and Iqbal Maidan, once existed but was demolished by the government to widen the road. Consequently, two gates to the complex were also demolished along with it.[110]

Nawab Sikandar Jahan Begum constructed the Moti Masjid, also known as the Pearl Mosque, using a combination of white marble and red sandstone. The mosque was designed as an imitation of the Jama Masjid located in Delhi[111]. Situated in the historic core of Bhopal alongside other significant Begum tructures, the mosque occupies an elevated position on a southward sloping terrain, overlooking the Bada Talab. Positioned on a terrace, the mosque faces the west in order to align with the direction of the Kaaba.

Architecturally, Moti Masjid reflects the later Mughal style. It consists of a square Sahn (courtyard) with colonnaded cloisters along three sides, while a covered prayer hall occupies the western side, with basements underneath the north, west, and south sides. The main entrance is a striking large Iwan located on the eastern wall, accessed through the garden within the premises. Additionally, two smaller Iwans provide entry into the mosque courtyard from the north and south roads. These gateways feature multi-foil arches framing the entrance, with arched niches on either side.

The Sahn is enclosed by arcaded cloisters supported by ornamental circular columns and rectangular bases. Two ablution tanks are located near the eastern corners of the courtyard. Chhatris mark the peripheral corners of the mosque, and the parapets both

Moti Masjid

inside and outside the mosque are adorned with carved merlons. The prayer hall is flanked by two octagonal three-tiered minarets topped with Chhatris at its western corners.

Inside the prayer hall, which is divided into eleven bays running north-south and two aisles running east-west, a series of carved double columns provide support. The external side of the prayer hall remains unadorned, while the interior is characterised by intricate carvings and relief work. The Qibla wall features arched niches at each bay, with the central bay housing an elaborately articulated semicircular Mihrab.

The prayer hall is crowned by three bulbous onion domes clad in white marble, situated on high drums. The central dome is slightly larger and elevated compared to the other two. Additionally, a smaller half-dome rests above the entrance of the prayer hall.

In terms of construction materials, the mosque predominantly utilises red sandstone, likely sourced from quarries near Rewa and Chanderi. Marble is used as cladding on the sandstone base, primarily in the prayer hall and domes. Lime is employed as a later addition to strengthen the structure, while the entrance doorway is crafted from wood and iron.

The Khirni Wala Maidan Complex, also known as Iqbal Maidan, is a large area measuring 210m x 120m, spacious enough to accommodate the entire population of the city. Within this complex, the presence of Moti Mahal Palace divides the space into two courtyards of unequal sizes: Khirniwala Maidan and Sadar Manzil Maidan. Positioned at the head of Khirniwala Maidan, Moti Masjid played a significant role in establishing Bhopal's new royal enclave, which consisted of imperial and sub-imperial palace complexes. Notable among these were Sikandar Begum's Moti Mahal, along with other palaces such as Shaukat Mahal, Zeenat Mahal, Humayun Manzil, and Hamid Manzil. The maidan was renamed to Iqbal Maidan after the noted Urdu Poet Iqbal stayed here during his visit to Bhopal.

The impressive Gate of Bab-e-Sikandari connects Iqbal Maidan to Pari Ghat below, visually linking Moti Mahal and Gauhar Mahal and creating a cohesive architectural ensemble. Pari Ghat served as an access point to the upper lake, specifically catering to women bathers and worshippers. However, due to the construction of the VIP road, Pari Ghat is no longer connected to the upper lake. Near Iqbal Maidan, one can find Shifa Manzil (Mahal Madarul Maham), which was constructed in the 1840s CE. This palace served as the residence of the Wazir of Nawab Sikander Jehan Begum, Munshi Jamaluddin Khan Madarul Maham Riyasat Bhopal.

The garden, known by the name Farhat Afza, literally meaning "The Increase of Delight", belonged to Sikandar Jahan Begum. This picturesque garden boasted a diverse array of fruit-bearing trees and vibrant flowers. Additionally, within its premises, an exquisite mosque, the garden featured wells and walls, enhancing its functionality. Sikandar Jahan Begum died on 30 October 1868 CE at the age 51 in Moti Mahal. Her burial is also situated in a tastefully designed monument adorned with the grave.[112]

The Jehangiria Higher Secondary School, erected in the 1850s CE, is situated in the Sheher-e-Khas area. It is a two-storey brick and mortar building adorned with an intricately carved false balcony projection over the entrance. The facade features cusp arches with a semicircular design, along with rectangular openings and triangular and semi-circular pediments. Inside, there is a spacious courtyard, but some additions on one side are not in harmony with the original structure.

The ground floor is covered with iron girders supporting stone slabs, while the first floor utilises jack arches. The construction of this building, likely intended for educational purposes, took place during the reign of Sikandar Jahan Begum, utilising materials such as brick, stone, stucco work, and timber. The monument, although unprotected, is in a reasonably well-preserved state.

Masjid Umrao Dulha, built in 1860 CE, is situated in Shehr-e-Khas. The title "Umrao Dulha" was bestowed upon General Baqi Mohammad Khan, the youngest son of the renowned Bakshi Bahadur Mohammad Khan. He was the first husband of Sikandar Jahan Begum's daughter, ShahJehan Begum.

The mosque is made of brick with stone sills and lintels. Pointed arches divide the prayer hall from the courtyard, and a crown is placed on the parapet at the entrance to signify its royal association. Inside the mosque, there is a Qbr (grave). Over time, the mosque has undergone extensive renovations and extensions, and currently, only the original minarets are visible from the outside. The entire structure is now covered with glass windows, giving it a modern appearance. The ownership of the mosque falls under the MP Waqf Board.[113]

Masjid Saifi is situated in the Sheher-e-Khas locality and was built during Nawab Sikandar Jahan Begum's reign. It is a spacious mosque featuring three large domes. These fluted domes rest on an elongated neck drum and are adorned with pinnacles. Additionally, there are four minarets placed at each corner of the prayer hall. The Mehrab, an architectural niche indicating the direction of prayer, is recessed into the back wall and covered with a half dome.

The mosque was constructed using brick and lime as the primary materials. Presently, it falls under the ownership of the MP Waqf Board, though it lacks protection. However, Masjid Saifi is reasonably well-preserved and maintained.[114]

Located near Jumerati Gate, Mandir Kamali was established on an eight-acre Bagh (garden) gifted to a sadhu named Narayan Das by Nawab Sikander Jehan Begum in 1852 CE. It is believed that the temple was constructed sometime after this event. The temple is designed around a courtyard, featuring colonnade halls accessed through a semi-circular arched entrance. The stone columns rest on square bases and display multi-foliated arches facing the courtyard. The temple's prominent fluted Shikhara is adorned with a horizontal band decorated with inverted lotus over Amlaka and Kalasa. Additionally, there are four Chhatris positioned at the four corners of the Shikhara. A small alabaster Chhatri embellished with leaf and flower carvings graces the centre of the courtyard.

Constructed using a combination of stone, brick, and mortar, the temple lacks protection from any governmental agency. However, it is well-maintained by The Mandir Trust and remains in good preservation, with some new additions made over time.[115]

◇◇◇◇◇◇◇◇◇◇◇◇◇◇◇◇◇◇◇◇◇

12

NAWAB SHAHJEHAN BEGUM (1868-1901 CE)

Nawab ShahJehan Begum, who had succeeded nominally on 11th April 1845 CE, was now again, on 16th November 1868 CE, invested as ruler of Bhopal. Her daughter Sultan Jahan, who had been born on 27 *Zikat* 1274 AH (9th July 1858 CE), was declared heir-apparent. On 13 *Safar* 1284 AH (16th July 1867 CE), Nawab Baqi Mohammad Khan died.

ShahJehan at once proceeded to follow in her mother's footsteps and continue the reforms in the administration. She had, upon the death of her husband, come out of pardah, which immensely facilitated her conduct of affairs.

The postal system was started in Bhopal in 1862 CE. Post offices, with peons and runners, were opened in each Tehsil, and a Head Office with supervisory power, was opened in Bhopal. In December 1869 CE, she visited Calcutta and was introduced to His Royal Highness the Duke of Edinburgh. Besides many minor improvements, ShahJehan had a plane table survey of the state made for revenue purposes, to take the place of the old jarib survey made in her mother's time.

In May 1871 CE, Begum married Maulvi Sayad Sidiq Hussin. The Maulvi had been in the service of the state for 17 years, having served as Munshi to Sikandar Begum, who had promoted him to keeper of the state archives and then head of the educational department. After the marriage, the Maulvi was accorded the title of Nawab Wala Jah Amir-ul-mulk and a personal salute of 17 guns, with the right to receive and return the visits of British officials. After her second marriage, the Begum again retired behind the pardah. In 1872 CE, she was made a GCSI In AH 1291 (1874 CE), her daughter Sultan Jahan married one of her own clan, Sultan Ahmad Ali Khan, descended from Sarda Mir Kali Khan, a brother of Khan Mohammad Khan, great-grandfather of the founder of the state. Her Highness attended the Imperial Assemblage held at Delhi in 1877 CE, receiving a banner and medal.

ShahJehan, in 1879 CE, obtained sanction for the establishment of an opium agency in Bhopal. In 1880 CE, she agreed to defray the cost of the railway from Hoshangabad to Bhopal. In 1891 CE, land for the Bhopal — Ujjain line was ceded, and in the same year, all transit duties on salt were abolished, with the government paying compensation of 10,000 rupees per annum. After her second marriage, dissensions arose between ShahJehan and her daughter, which were fomented by the Nawab, until, in 1884 CE, a regular impasse had been reached and the Government of India was obliged to intervene and deprive the Nawab of all his honours, titles, and salute. He died of dropsy in 1800 CE. The state was henceforth managed by Begum herself, assisted by a minister. In 1891 CE, Lord Lansdowne visited Bhopal, the first occasion of a Viceroy's visit to the state, which was signalled by the exemption of Her Highness the Begum and her successors from presenting a *nazar* (complimentary gift) in interviews with the Viceroy. A hospital was open for the female subjects of Bhopal on the occasion of his visit. It was called "Lady Lansdowne Hospital". New wings were added to this hospital on 21st May 1892 CE, on the anniversary of the birthday of Her Imperial Majesty. Two viceroys have since visited the state: Lord Elgin in 1895 CE and Lord Curzon in 1899 CE. On 1st July 1897 CE, British Indian coinage was adopted.

Envisioned by Nawab Shahjehan Begum, ShahJehanabad is a walled settlement in the old city area. This was a walled settlement where Taj Mahal Palace, Taj-ul-Masajid, Benazir Palace, cascading lakes, and other residential areas were situated. People from the northern part of the city were lured to buy land in this area. Begum gifted free lands to people and, in some cases, gave people money to build houses. Thus, quite a large portion of the locality eventually became inhabited. Around the Taj Mahal were localities known as Nawab Manzil, Baramahal, Amir Ganj, Kaisarganj, Mughalpura, and Khawaspura. The houses in these localities were laid out on a uniform plan to meet the requirements of all classes of people, from the members of the ruling family to the people in ordinary walks of life. Over time, Shahjehanabad has become a densely populated area. The fortification wall is nowhere to be seen, but a few gates are still standing. The structures in the localities like Baramahal and Nawab Manzil have been modified to such an extent that the original fabric is

Taj Mahal Palace

nowhere to be seen. The open spaces in between these areas have been encroached upon, making it almost impossible to trace the original layout of ShahJehanabad.

Nawab Shahjehan Begum constructed the Taj Mahal Palace for herself, with its construction taking 13 years from 1871 to 1884 CE. It stood among the world's largest palaces during that era and was initially known as Raj Mahal ("royal palace"). The British Resident at Bhopal was highly impressed by its architecture and recommended renaming it Taj Mahal in reference to the Taj Mahal in Agra, built by the Begum's namesake, ShahJehan. Following the suggestion, the palace was renamed Taj Mahal, and the completion of the building was celebrated with a three-year-long event called Jashn-e Taj Mahal.

Dakhil Darwaza, located around 100m in front of the Taj Mahal Palace, serves as the primary entrance to the Taj Mahal Complex. Constructed in the 1880s CE, it was built alongside the Taj Mahal Palace. Due to its location on the railway station road, all guests were directed through this gate, making it the main entrance to the palace complex. Additionally, there are two other gateways adjacent to the palace entrance. The first one, called Teen Mohre, is relatively simpler in design, featuring three passageways, and was constructed in 1884 CE as part of the Taj Mahal Complex. The second gate of Teen Mohre is a two-storey structure situated on the south-east edge of the Taj Mahal Palace.

The Taj Mahal's architecture is a blend of British, French, Mughal, Arabic, and Hindu influences. The palace stands on a plinth covering a vast area and comprises 120 rooms, including a hall of mirrors (Sheesh Mahal) and the Sawan-Bhadon pavilion. The entrance gate is an impressive seven-storied structure adorned with jharokhas and a three-storied cusped archway. It is a square plinth measuring 15m x 15m, rising 20m high, with crown parapets and pavilions at its four corners. The gate's shutters are reinforced with metal sheets featuring 15 cm long spikes. The gateway's dome is renowned as the second largest after Gol Gumbaz. Notably, the Bagghi drawn by eight horses can manoeuvre within the gateway's covered dome.[116]

A complex maze of corridors interconnects the various sections of the palace. The central large courtyard sits two floors above the entrance dome. Many parts of the palace open into this courtyard, and its centrepiece is a walk-in fountain known as Sawan Bhadon Sahan. The name derives from the copper balls floating on the water-filled roof, creating a thunder-like sound. The fountain's carved stone structure serves both as a sculpture piece and a functioning fountain. Historical maps indicate the presence of an elaborate char bagh surrounding the fountain.

The palace's design cleverly utilises the proximity of Motia Lake to its southern side. Large underground air ducts circulate the cool air from the tank into the palace. The side facing the tank remains open, featuring baradaries and Diwan-e-Aam. The surfaces of this section are adorned with glass inlay work and fresco paintings. Pointed arches and cobbled stone embellish other areas of the palace, while wooden carving, tin cuttings, and stucco work are additional prominent features. This palace is part of a larger complex of buildings near three lakes, which also includes the Benazir Palace, serving as the Begum's summer palace, and the Taj-ul-Masjid Mosque.

Following India's partition in 1947 CE, Nawab Hamidullah Khan allowed Sindhi refugees to take refuge in the palace, and they resided there for approximately four years before relocating to Bairagarh. Unfortunately, the palace incurred some damage during this period. After India gained independence, certain members of the royal family of Bhopal stayed at the palace initially but eventually moved away due to financial constraints, hindering the necessary repairs.

In 2005 CE, the Government of Madhya Pradesh honoured the palace by declaring it a state heritage monument, prompting the state archaeology department to carry out partial restoration work. By 2008 CE, significant portions of the palace complex collapsed. However, in 2011 CE, it was denotified. Presently, the government has plans to transfer the property to the tourism department for its transformation into a heritage hotel.

Situated in ShahJehanabad, the mosque stands as one of the beautifully crafted structures of the former Bhopal state. Made of sandstone, it boasts two elegant minarets crowned with dome-covered chhatris, adorned with slender flutes running vertically on the exterior. The entrance gateway features two smaller chhatris at the ends of the crenellations on the parapet. Munshi Hussain was the mastermind behind the construction of this mosque.

The sandstone structure is relatively well-preserved and maintained by the Mohalla Committee. However, the ownership lies with the Waqf Board of Madhya Pradesh. Over time, unsympathetic additions and extensions have altered the originality of the mosque.[117]

Noor Mahal, the palace of Nawab Siddhique Hasan, who was the second husband of Nawab Shahjehan Begum, was connected to the Taj Mahal Palace by a tramway, leading to the popular nickname "Thele Wali Sadak" for Kaiser Embankment. Presently, only the entrance gateway and a reconstructed mosque are visible, as the rest of Noor Mahal, a brick mortar construction, has disappeared. The site is not protected and is under private ownership.[118]

ShahJehanabad, the historical city, boasted three terraced lakes interconnected in a cascading manner. The largest lake, Motia Talab, lay surrounded by the Taj-ul-Masjid on its south side and Taj Mahal Palace on the north side. This lake served as a reservoir for rainwater collected from nearby hills and city drains. Situated below Motia Talab, at a 15-metre lower level, was Noor Mahal Talab, also known as Siddique Hassan Talab, named after Nawab Shahjehan Begum's husband. Stretching from Noor Mahal in the south to Dakhil Darwaza in the north, this lake played a vital role in the water system of ShahJehanabad. The smallest of the three cascading lakes was Husain Baksh Lake, commonly called Husain Bakshi Ki Talliya, named after the royal courtman Munshi Hussain Baksh.

The elite of ShahJehanabad preferred to build their palaces and residences along these lakes. The uppermost lake, Motia Talab, spanned an area of 230 m x 230 m; the intermediate level lake, Noor Mahal Talab, covered a space of 175 m x 230 m; and the lowest lake, Munshi Hussaini Talab, extended over an area of 115 m x 230 m. These lakes depended on surface run-off water from seasonal rains. To regulate the water levels and maintain balance, an additional reservoir was constructed to the north of ShahJehanabad. The system consisted of brick-lined vaulted drains that collected and directed water to the lakes, passing through important buildings before reaching the Talabs. These channels were ingeniously transformed into fountains, cascades, and stone streams with intricate carvings. Rose water or 'kewra' was added to the water to cool and refresh the air, creating a delightful environment.[119]

Yateem Khana, also known as Dar-ul-Shafqat ShahJehani, is a Muslim orphanage house located in ShahJehanabad, in the vicinity of Taj-ul-Masjid. It was constructed during the reign of ShahJehan Begum. The architectural style of the monument is a blend of Indian and Islamic

Motia Talab, Noor Mahal Talab & Husain Bakshi Ki Talliya

elements, featuring two stories with a front view that showcases a slight concave curvature. The structure stands on simple brackets, supporting a baranda with multiple Mihrabs. Additionally, the building is adorned with a row of pediments, cornices, and parapets on both sides. The use of sandstone in its construction adds to its historical charm.

Yateem Khana houses a separate school for boys and girls that are still running. The orphanage for boys still operates within Yateem Khana, providing education from nursery to twelfth grade. For girls, a similar facility exists in the Sadar Manzil complex, near Humayun Manzil, housing the Hamidia Higher Secondary Girls School.

The ownership of the site is under the Wakf Board, ensuring its religious and social significance is preserved. However, there have been reports of cracks and water seepage, but regular repairs are carried out to maintain its structural integrity. Despite its historical importance, Yateem Khana is currently unprotected, leading to concerns about its conservation.

Taj-Ul-Masajid, known as 'The Crown of Mosques', holds the distinction of being the largest mosque in India. Spanning approximately 23,000 square metres, it was intended to be the biggest mosque in all of Asia during its construction. The initiative to build this mosque was undertaken during the reign of Nawab Shahjehan Begum in 1877 CE. It is believed that Begum's marriage to Nawab Siddique Hassan, a devout follower of Islam, ignited her religious fervour and inspired her to construct a grand mosque, thereby establishing Bhopal as a centre for Islamic teachings.

Similar to other mosques in Bhopal, Taj-Ul-Masajid features three entrances, with the main entrance situated along the Kaiser embankment. Elevated on a lofty plinth, the main gateway can be reached through a series of semicircular stairs. The entryway is adorned with a triple-height cusped arch, flanked by niches on either side. The gateway itself has an octagonal shape and incorporates a balcony with intricately carved stone jali serving as a parapet, supported by stone brackets. Crenellations adorn the upper edges of all eight walls of the gateway, and atop it, eight slender minarets rise gracefully.

Passing through the gateway, one enters the central open courtyard, which encompasses a wazoo tank at its centre. This expansive

Taj-Ul-Masajid

courtyard spans an area of approximately 17,000 square metres and can accommodate over 100,000 people at once. Surrounding the courtyard, corridors on three sides house various rooms, while the first floor features two large pavilions, each topped with a domed chhatri, positioned on the northeast and southeast corners of the mosque. Finally, at the western edge of the courtyard, one can find the main prayer hall and the minarets.

Perched atop a hill, the Idgah serves as a designated prayer ground for offering namaz. During the 19th century CE, Bhopal witnessed a rapid increase in its Muslim population, leading to a shortage of mosques, particularly during Friday prayers. To address this issue, ShahJehan Begum, the ruler at the time, envisioned constructing the largest mosque in the world. Initially, she selected the location of Idgah Hills, previously known as Mehboobgarh, for this purpose. However, due to inadequate access to a sufficient water source, she altered her plan and relocated the mosque to its present site in ShahJehanabad, where Taj-Ul-Masajid now stands. Subsequently, the area initially designated as Idgah was eventually developed, and in 1898 CE, ShahJehan Begum oversaw its construction.[120]

The Alexandria school, also known as Darul Kaza, is located in ShahJehanabad, behind Taj-Ul-Masajid. It is a long vaulted structure featuring 45 crown-like parapets situated along the ridge of the vault. The building is otherwise plain, consisting of rooms lined up in a row. Constructed using stone, the building boasts long arches with brick-made pointed serrates resembling crowns. Originally, the purpose of the building was to serve as a school affiliated with the Jhansi Board, as indicated by an engraved prose inscription attributed to ShahJehan Begum, who was responsible for its construction. Currently, the premises house the Madhya Pradesh Waqf Board and several other government offices.

Built in 1875 CE, the Benazir Palace is located in ShahJehanabad, close to the Taj Mahal Palace and Taj-Ul-Masajid. It served as the summer residence for Shahjehan Begum and is accessed through the impressive Benazir Gate. Adjacent to the palace, you can find the picturesque Benazir Ghats on the banks of Motia Talab, featuring pillared structures reminiscent of aqueducts.

The palace itself has an 'H' shape, with two arms extending towards Motia Talab, ending in octagonal pavilions. Inside, there was a water channel adorned with fountains. The western side houses a stunning hammam (bathhouse) with exquisite water architecture and stone carvings inspired by the Sawan Bhadon Sahan style found in the Taj Mahal Complex. The interiors are adorned with slender cast iron pillars and brackets, likely imported from outside India, showcasing their beauty. Notably, the palace boasts intricate woodwork with

Benazir Palace

coloured glass accents on its door shutters, highlighting the exceptional craftsmanship. The Benazir Palace served as both a pleasure pavilion in the garden and a summer residence for the begum. It was also designed to accommodate state dignitaries. From the palace, one could enjoy a view of the expanding landscape to the east, overlooking three water bodies: the uppermost Motia Talab, the middle Noor Talab, and the lowermost Munshi Hussain Talab. The palace's surroundings featured green stepped terraces, lively fountains, and a series of steps and plinths descending to the water.[121]

The adjacent ground was used for ceremonial purposes, and a three-entrance gateway was constructed for royal entries. This gateway boasted elegant Falaknuma designs, including canopies at the top. Unfortunately, a fire accident destroyed two out of the six canopies. During that time, the archaeology department was housed on the first storey of the gateway.

In 1908 CE, Lord and Lady Minto stayed at the Benazir Palace during their visit to the city. Later, in 1929 CE, Mahatma Gandhi also visited Bhopal and was hosted at the same palace. During his stay, the decor of the palace was transformed, with all upholstery, curtains, sofas, and chair covers being changed to white "Khadi." Gandhi expressed his hope that this style of interior decoration would continue even after he left.[122]

Unfortunately, over time, the palace has been neglected, and its original structure has suffered damage due to unsympathetic expansions. Presently, some parts of the palace are used for film shooting, indicating a change in its usage and significance.

Pari Bazaar, also known as Parween Manzil, was a spacious enclosed area featuring a single formal entrance gate with shutters. It is situated across from Babe Ali Gate and was constructed during the late nineteenth century under the rule of Shahjehan Begum. With the aim of enhancing the economic well-being of women, Begum established this marketplace called Meena Bazaar and bestowed upon it the name Parween Manzil. The construction of this market entailed an expenditure of 3 lakh rupees, and it was exclusively designated for women to engage in trade activities.

Gulshan-e-Alam (Gol Ghar)

Gol Ghar, situated near Bab-e-Ali Stadium in ShahJehanabad, was built in 1885 CE. It is also known as Gulshan-e-Alam and stands as a remarkable architectural gem constructed on a circular stone base. The concept behind Gol Ghar, according to Architect SM Hussain from the Nawab family lineage, was to provide assistance to impoverished individuals who preferred to maintain their anonymity. This idea inspired the creation of 24 cusped arch entrances encircling the structure, leading to a circular pathway that guides visitors to an inner circular hall featuring 12 doors. The entry doors are adorned with coloured glass imported from Europe, crowned by exquisitely crafted coloured glass fanlights with wooden security grills. The circular pathway is a single-storey structure supported by I-beam sections with a stone slab.

The inner hall, a double-height chamber, is capped by an onion-shaped dome. The inner surface of the dome showcases intricate fresco paintings in shades of red, orange, brown, yellow, and green. During the reign of the begum, the hall was illuminated by a chandelier imported from France. The terrace of Gol Ghar is circular and partially covered with corrugated sheets supported by slender wooden pillars. The parapet of Gol Ghar boasts a unique design, featuring intricately crafted individual elements resembling flowers placed closely together in repetition. According to tales, when Begum Shahjehan decided to present a gift to Queen Victoria of England, she added a personal touch. Numerous weaver birds were released inside Gol Ghar, along with precious cloth rags, silver and gold threads, and other jewels. Over time, the birds wove numerous nests using these materials, and the finest nest was then gifted to Queen Victoria.

Initially, Gol Ghar was encompassed by a Persian Garden, which lost its identity and beauty over time. The garden used to host special band performances every evening for the begum's enjoyment. Additionally, the Gol Ghar complex included a Payga, a set of rooms utilised by staff for living and leisure. Following Independence, Gol Ghar served as the office for the Income Tax Department and Railway Police Department. Currently, it functions as a museum exhibiting a collection of photographs and artefacts from the era of the begum. Gol Ghar is a protected monument under the jurisdiction of the Directorate of Archaeology, Archives and Museums in Bhopal.

During her reign, Shahjehan Begum undertook the expansion of the city of Bhopal towards its northern side. In honour of her own name, she named the newly extended area ShahJehanabad. To ensure the security and fortification of the city, Shahjehan Begum commissioned the construction of seven secondary gateways. These gateways were strategically placed and served different purposes. They were known as the Military Gate, Police Gate, Post Office Gate, Bab-e-Karbala (Bhopal) Gate, Bab-e-Ali Gate, and others.

As time passed and the city continued to grow, the decision was made to demolish the walls that once surrounded ShahJehanabad. However, the gateways, which had become iconic landmarks, were preserved and remained standing even after the walls were taken down. These gateways serve as landmarks and a reminder of ShahJehan Begum's vision for the city.

Bhopal Gate, also known as Bab-e-Karbala, was one of the gates constructed by Nawab Shahjehan Begum in Bhopal. This square-shaped gate featured chambered corners and a pointed arched vault for passage. It stood tall with two storeys.

The architectural style of Bhopal Gate was influenced by the Indo-Islamic tradition. The pointed arches, characteristic of Islamic architecture, were prominently incorporated into its design. Additionally, the front side of the gate showcased intricate Jali work, inspired by the Rajputana style. The gate was meticulously crafted using Dholpur stone, which was carefully cut and laid in levelled courses. Locally available materials were skillfully used to bind the stone together.

When the Bourbon family, descendants of Louis XIV, visited Bhopal, a French influence was introduced into various architectural structures, including Bhopal Gate. At the top of the parapet, a club-shaped fence was added, showcasing this additional touch.

Over time, the gate found new purposes. It served as the location for the library of Hamidia College, situated right in front of it. Later, it was declared the Martyr Gate, paying tribute to Major Ajay Prasad and numerous other freedom fighters. A replica of a gun was placed on the raised platform at the centre of the gateway to honour the freedom fighters from the Bhopal region. Additionally, the gate features an "Amar Jawan Jyoti" (Eternal Flame) fuelled by gas, symbolising the sacrifice and valour of the martyrs.[123]

The Police Gate, situated at the entrance of Chhavni, was constructed by Shahjehan Begum during the period of 1870-1885 CE. This historical gate held significant importance, as it housed the living quarters for army personnel on one side, while the other side was dedicated to stables for elephants and horses. The architectural design of the gate showcased various elements, including onion domes, trefoil and pointed arches, windows, gates, and vaults. Additionally, a guard's room was incorporated within the gate itself.

Following India's independence, the purpose of this location shifted, and it was transformed into a police canteen. However, presently, the canteen is no longer in use. During its construction, the materials utilised included stone, brick, and cement plaster. Iron was also employed for reinforcement purposes. Notably, a wooden gate once existed within the gateway but has since been demolished. The municipal corporation took responsibility for renovating the gate on three separate occasions.[124]

The Bab-e-Ali Gate, located in ShahJehanabad, stands along Aali Manzil road in the neighborhood of Pari Bazar. This remarkable architectural structure features a circular arched design, adorned with a triangular balcony. Serving as the gateway to the Bab-e-Ali ground, it holds historical significance in its purpose and construction. On either side of the gate, one can find protruding rooms characterised by half circular pillars and elegant arches, adding to its grandeur. Originally, the Bab-e-Ali Gate was erected with the specific intention of prohibiting the entry of men and boys above the age of 9 into the women's club that existed during that period. The construction features a timber frame adorned with either brick or Bousillage, which consists of a mixture of mud, moss, and animal hair. The implementation incorporates slim wooden columns, while the living quarters within the gate have been elevated above the ground level.[125]

The Sultania Infantry Gate, also known as the Regiment Gate or Military Gate, is a historic structure that was constructed in the late nineteenth century CE. Its architectural design bears a striking resemblance to the police gate, featuring similar elements and characteristics. With its double arches, adorned with a cusped arch on the outer side and an ogee arch on the inner side, the Sultania Infantry Gate showcases a remarkable architectural vocabulary. Crafted from finely dressed stones, the gate is further enhanced by the presence of dome-shaped chhatris adorning each of its four corners. In the middle, the gate boasts a crown-like parapet, which is emblematic of the distinctive Bhopal architectural style.

Historical records indicate that the Sultania Infantry Gate served as one of the entrances to the walled city of ShahJehanabad. Its strategic location facilitated monitoring of the surrounding areas, allowing for enhanced security measures. As time went on, the gate underwent adaptations to accommodate various needs. Notably, the interior rooms of the gate were repurposed and used as classrooms. The presence of remnants such as chalkboards and a science lab provides tangible evidence of this transformation. Furthermore, residential quarters have been constructed in close proximity to the gate. However, the gate is owned by the Public Works Department

Shaukat Mahal

(PWD).[126,127]

Shaukat Mahal, an architectural marvel, was constructed during ShahJehan Begum's reign as a wedding gift for her mother Sikander Jehan Begum. Functioning as a residential palace for Sikander Jehan Begum, the building also serves as an entrance gate within the quadrangle, like many other palaces added by Shahjehan Begum. The intervention was also made by Qudsia Begum as she, as mentioned in the book *Bhopal* by the state Archaeology Department, invited French architects for its design and construction and also developed a rose garden in front of the palace.

The design is attributed to the Bourbons of Bhopal, descendants of the French King, which is evident in the church-like inputs and crown on the facade. The palace is an integral part of the famous royal quadrangle of Bhopal surrounding the Iqbal Maidan. The architectural features are a unique blend of Islamic and European styles, with stone carvings, jaali, coloured glass work, stucco work, wood carvings, and chhatris. The palace boasts an Italian fresco technique of painting, which is rare in India, with fine examples of paintings using colours like black, red, grey, sky blue, yellow, and pink.

The primary construction material used was brick and mortar, and the palace also featured iron and copper fountains. Shaukat

Zeenat Mahal

Mahal is currently under private ownership and unprotected by any governmental agencies, leading to its vulnerability to further deterioration. The palace's unique architectural features highlight the importance of urgent preservation efforts to safeguard it for future generations.

Zeenat Mahal was another significant addition made by Nawab Shahjehan Begum to the Khirni Wala Maidan Complex, complementing the quadrangle's edges and giving it its current dimensions. Like its neighbour Shaukat Mahal, Zeenat Mahal contributed to the complex's cohesive architectural structure, with open spaces within the building. Despite some differences in details, it visually stands apart while still enhancing the unity and overall expression of the quadrangle.

This palace showcases a blend of Islamic and European architecture, evident in elements such as pediments above the door openings, linear plaster lines, and flatter facade wings. Unlike Shaukat Mahal, it utilises stone slabs as a building material. Despite its ownership in the hands of the Public Works Department, the palace is facing deterioration due to negligence.

Hira Masjid, constructed by Nawab Siddique Hassan, the second husband of Nawab Sultan Jahan Begum, in 1890s CE, is a hidden gem within the Iqbal Maidan complex. Situated between Zeenat Mahal and Sheesh Mahal and facing east-west, the mosque is presumed to be named "Hira Masjid" because it is built with marble. It's interesting to note that before Hira Masjid's addition, there was a gap between Sheesh Mahal and Zeenat Mahal.

The Sheesh Mahal is situated on the edge of the Khirniwala Maidan. Its large gateway opens into the Khirniwala quadrangle, featuring a double-arched design with cusped arch and plaster moulding. The main focus is a jharokha projection made of carved timber. This two-story palace is built around two courtyards and exhibits Doric capitals over plain circular columns, along with triangular pediment designs created with stucco work over the rectangular openings within semi-circular arches. Circular balconies and heavy cornices are among its other features.

One wing of the building, which obstructed the view of Moti Masjid from the quadrangle and contained two gateways for traffic movement, was demolished to accommodate increasing traffic. Notably, the renowned Urdu poet Iqbal is said to have stayed here during his visit to Bhopal.

The primary building materials used for the structure were stone slabs and lime plaster, with additional materials like iron and wood. Unfortunately, the remaining parts of the palace are currently in a poor state of preservation.

Built in 1898 CE by Shahjehan Begum, Sadar Manzil has a special place in the history of Bhopal. During the reign of Shahjehan Begum, it was used as a palace for Nawab Sultan Jahan Begum. When Nawab Sultan Jahan Begum took charge of the Bhopal Principality, she left Sadar Manzil and made her own new walled city named Ahmedabad. Sadar Manzil was changed into a Darbar hall, where people used to come with their problems to discuss them with the Begum. Sadar Manzil witnessed the crowning ceremony of Sultan Jahan Begum on July 4, 1901 CE. After independence, the Government Municipal Corporation Office was run from here, before it was shifted to the ISBT.

The gate of Sadar Manzil is relatively simple in design. It has a double-height multifoliate arch entry. A large gateway of the palace opens into the Sadar Manzil quadrangle. The double arch gateway

Sadar Manzil

has a cusped arch and plaster moulding. The palace is a two-storeyed structure built around a courtyard. The fountains, merlons, stone brackets, and fresco painting with gold paint on acanthus leaf capitals and extensive use of lime stucco plaster mouldings on the walls is very much like the work in the Taj Mahal Palace.

The materials used in the construction are stone, brick, lime, wood and metals like iron and copper. Unsympathetic painting, extensions, neglect, and lack of a technically sound conservation program has resulted in the poor state of the building.

Hamid Manzil, also known as Sultan Manzil, is situated between Sadar Manzil and Shaukat Mahal. The palace is visually separated from Shaukat Mahal by the Moti Mahal gate. This structure is part of the Sadar Manzil quadrangle. Nawab Hamidullah, the youngest son of Sultan Jahan Begum, was born in this palace. The front gate is the only visible feature from the Sadar Manzil quadrangle, but there is a courtyard accessible through a passage leading to the palace's interior. The palace's elevation features pointed and horseshoe arches, while the hammam inside still functions and has decorative carvings on its walls. Presently, the palace is owned by Mr. Anwar Khan and is used as a wedding venue. Although it lacks protection, it remains in

Hamid Manzil

relatively good condition due to renovations and restoration efforts.

Maqbara Nawab Siddique Hassan is situated near Bara Bagh, and it stands as one of the most captivating structures in Bhopal. This white alabaster cenotaph is located at the intersection of Hamidia Road and Berasia Road, elevated on a high platform made of sandstone adorned with delicate carvings and moulded edges. The Maqbara is enveloped on all four sides by intricate jali work, with openings on two sides. Turrets and finials project from the screen, adding to its architectural charm. The Qbr, or tomb, is crafted in marble, and there is no roofing over it.

Nawab Siddique Hassan became the second husband of ShahJehan Begum on May 8, 1871 CE, and he was bestowed with the title of Nawab Wala Jah Amir-Ul-Mulk along with a personal salute of seventeen guns. He was a prolific writer, authoring numerous books, some of which focused on Jihad. However, in 1884 CE, the Viceroy stripped him of all his honours, titles, and salute. Nawab Siddhique Hasan passed away in 1890 CE due to dropsy. An inscription on the

Maqbara Nawab Siddique Hassan

cenotaph extends wishes of paradise for him. The structure itself is made of marble and alabaster and has been well-preserved over the years, continuing to hold its appeal.

The Lady Lansdowne Hospital, later renamed Sultania Jenana Hospital, was constructed in the Shehr e Khas area during the reign of Shahjehan Begum. The foundation stone for the hospital was laid on May 26, 1892 CE, by Lady Lansdowne. The building features a dressed stone structure, similar to many other constructions from that era. Circular dressed pillars and pointed arches can be accessed via steps running along the entire length of the facade. The upper floors were once covered by a sloping roof adorned with terracotta tiles. However, since the 1950s CE, extensive expansions and additions have been made to the building. Opposite Sultania Zenana Hospital lies the public garden called Yadgar-e-Shahjehani, which was built in the 1890s CE. The monument is now under government ownership.

The baradari, a component of the former palace that once stood on the premises, is an impressive structure made of sandstone.

Baradari at Shamla Hills

Featuring exquisite stone jali work, intricately carved pillars, and beautifully crafted Chhajjas (overhanging eaves), the baradari stands as a testament to the fine craftsmanship of its time. Despite lacking formal protection, the baradari remains in excellent condition, preserving its historical charm and significance.[128]

The Raj Bhawan formerly known as Lal Kothi, has a historical background dating back to the rule of Nawab Nazar Mohammad Khan (1816-1819 CE) when the Britishers appointed a Political Agent in Bhopal. To ensure security and effective governance, a British armed force was stationed at Sehore Cantt.

The area where the present Raj Bhawan stands was a military cantonment area, restricting private construction. In 1880 CE, Nawab Shahjehan Begum of Bhopal commissioned the construction of the Lal Kothi as a residence for British officers, giving it the name Lal Kothi due to its red China clay 'Kavelus' roof and predominant red colour. The building was made of dressed stone in typical colonial bungalow style with a colonnade verandah. For many years, it remained

Lal Kothi

the official residence of British Political Agents in Bhopal until India gained independence. Presently, this is the residence of the Governor of Madhya Pradesh.[129]

The Lal Kothi was built over an area of 15,423 sq. ft. (0.354 acres) and followed European architecture. The total cost of construction amounted to 72,878 Rupees, 3 annas, and 1 paisa. It is noteworthy that before the main building, a small mosque was constructed on the campus, as per the prevalent custom in the Muslim State of Bhopal, where the foundation stone for a mosque was laid first whenever any significant building was erected. The construction of Lal Kothi was supervised by Austate Cook, a French Engineer, who was posted as the water works engineer in Bhopal. The erstwhile Bhopal Government sought assistance from British and PWD authorities in decorating the Kothi with European influences.

13

NAWAB SULTAN JAHAN BEGUM (1901-1926 CE)

ShahJehan Begum died on 16th June 1901 CE, and was succeeded by Sultan Jahan Begum, or Sultan Kaikhusrau Jehan Begum. Her husband, the Nawab-consort, who had been granted the title of AQ died suddenly on 4th January 1902 CE. She was honoured with the Delhi Durbar gold medal in 1903 CE. In 1904 CE, Sultan Jahan made the pilgrimage to Mecca. In 1905 CE, she was presented to Their Royal Highnesses the Prince and Princess of Wales at Indore and received the at the hands of the Prince. The Begum personally conducted the administration of her state, assisted by *Nawab Mohammad Nasr-ul-Lah Khan,* her eldest son.

She was awarded the Knight Grand Commander of the Order of the Star of India (GCSI) in 1910 CE and the Companion of the Order of the Crown of India (CI) in 1911 CE. She had three sons: Mohammad *Nasr-ul-lah Khan,* born 4th December 1876 CE; Sahibzada; Colonel *Ubaid-ul-lah Khan,* born 3rd November 1878 CE; and Mohammad *Hamid-ul-lah Khan,* born 9th September 1894 CE.

Sultan Jahan, a great reformer in the tradition of her mother and grandmother, established free and compulsory primary education in 1918 CE and established several important educational institutions in Bhopal. During her time in power, she placed a special emphasis on public education, particularly female education. She increased the number of qualified teachers and constructed numerous technical institutes and schools. She was the Aligarh Muslim University's founding chancellor from 1920 CE until her death. She will be the only woman to hold the position of Chancellor of Aligarh Muslim University by the year 2020 CE. She was appointed in 1920 CE, making her the first woman to lead an Indian university.

In addition to being a reformer in the field of training, the Nawab Begum improved tax collection, the military, police, the legal executive, and the correctional facilities; extended farming; and built a broad water system and public works in the state. In addition, she initiated open municipal elections and established an Executive and Legislative State Council in 1922 CE.

She was the All-India Muslim Ladies' Association's president in 1914 CE. Ruler Sultan Jahan's essential heritage, however, was in the field of general wellbeing, as she spearheaded broad immunisation and inoculation programmes and further developed the water supply and norms of cleanliness and disinfection. She was a prolific author who wrote Hidayat uz-Zaujan, Sabil ul-Jinan, Tandurusti (Health), Bachchon-ki-Parwarish, Hidayat Timardari, and Maishat-o-Moasherat, among other books on education, health, and other subjects. She was the recipient of numerous honours and awards as a result of her numerous activities. The ruler of Bhopal enjoyed the title of Her Highness Nawab Begum and received a salute of 19 guns (21 within the limits of the state).

In 1926 CE, following a rule of 25 years, Begum Sultan Jahan surrendered the high position to her most youthful and justly enduring child, Hamidullah Khan. She passed away on 12th May 1930 at the age of 71.

Sultan Jahan Begum constructed Ahmedabad Palace in 1905 CE. Ahmedabad Palace showcased unique flavours of architecture in accordance with its contemporaries. Being the first building to use Italian marble, the construction of the Ahmedabad Palace depicts modern construction technologies. Also known as Qaser-e-Sultani, it was the new residence for Sultan Jahan Begum and her sons.

Sultan Jahan Begum built the palace for her own use. It is a double storied rectangular structure built in the modern style without much embellishment. Use of new material such as reinforced brick concrete as roofing material gives it a flat and plain look. This was the break from the highly embellished islamic style adopted by the previous rulers.

Circular pillars, porticos, and entrance vestibules are some of the new architectural vocabulary used in the building. However, it has not been able to escape Islamic elements of bhopal architecture such as

Ahmedabad Palace

parapet designs, carved stone brackets and pointed arch niches.

In 1905 CE, Sultan Jahan Begum oversaw the construction of Ahmedabad Palace, also known as Qaser-e-Sultani. This remarkable palace displayed a distinctive architectural style, setting it apart from its contemporaries. It held the distinction of being the first building in the region to incorporate Italian marble, showcasing modern construction technologies of that era. Serving as the new residence for Sultan Jahan Begum and her sons, the palace was specifically designed for her personal use.

The structure of Ahmedabad Palace is characterised by a double-storeyed rectangular design, adhering to a modern architectural approach with minimal ornamentation. Notably, the palace made use of innovative materials such as reinforced brick concrete for its roofing, resulting in a flat and unadorned appearance. This marked a departure from the highly embellished Islamic style embraced by the previous rulers of the region. Incorporating new architectural vocabulary, the palace featured circular pillars, porticos, and entrance vestibules. Despite its modern elements, Ahmedabad Palace retained some Islamic architectural elements that are characteristic of Bhopal's architectural heritage. These elements include parapet designs, carved stone brackets, and pointed arch niches, blending traditional influences with the contemporary style of the palace.

In the Ahmedabad Palace area, there is a cluster of bungalows including Mr. Wikar Bungalow, Karbala Kashiana Bungalow, 5 Karbala Bungalows, RTO Bungalow, and Bhoot Bangla Bungalow. These bungalows were constructed during the rule of Nawab Sultan Jahan Begum and subsequent periods. Designed in a colonial style, they were primarily intended for British officers.

The building that serves as the official residence of the Chief Minister of Madhya Pradesh is situated on the flat grounds of the Shamla Hills, and offers a picturesque view of Bada Talab. The entrance to the building features a colonnade portico consisting of circular pillars made of dressed stone and semi-circular arches. Inside, there is a central hall with a corridor, around which the rooms are arranged. On the first floor, the rooms and terrace provide a vantage point to the lake. The building's architectural elements suggest its similarly to the present Governor's House (Lal Kothi) and it remains in excellent

Chief Minister's House

condition and has undergone extensive additions and modifications over time to meet evolving needs.

Situated atop the Shamla Hills, the Jehan Numa Palace is an elegant structure constructed with dressed stones. The rooms are arranged around an open-air courtyard, and the entry is through a porch leading to a colonnade verandah. The front section of the building is double-storeyed, featuring rooms on the first floor. The palace, known as Jehan Numa, was built in 1890 CE during the rule of Nawab Sultan Jahan Begum, by her second son, General Obaidullah Khan, who served as the commander in chief of the Bhopal State forces. Initially, it served as a guest house and also housed the revenue office for the Jagirs.

After General Obaidullah Khan's demise in 1918 CE, the palace underwent several changes in occupation. During this period, his sons, Nawab Said Uz Zafar and Nawabzada Rashid Uz Zafar Khan, utilised it for official purposes, utilizing it as their secretariat. This continued until 1952 CE when the Government of India abolished all the Jagirs. Subsequently, the palace was rented out to the government and served as a student's hostel for a brief period, and later as the office of the Geological Survey of Madhya Pradesh until 1981 CE.

In 1981 CE, the grandsons of General Obaidullah Khan, who are the present owners of the property, decided to convert it into a heritage hotel. Due to regular use and efficient management by the hotel authorities, the palace has been excellently preserved, retaining its historic charm and grandeur.

Humayun Manzil, situated adjacent to Sadar Manzil, was constructed between 1918 and 1922 CE. This double-storeyed building is designed around a central courtyard, which features two levels, with the upper level adorned with intricate marble jali work. Inside, stone balconies, supported by carved stone brackets, project into the courtyard on all sides. The first facade boasts a cast iron parapet and cast iron pillars that support the balcony roof. The entrance to the building is through a heavy ornate wooden door embellished with metal spikes. The roof, constructed with brick and lime mortar, consists of stone slabs supported by wooden beams.

Initially, the complex was part of Sadar Manzil but is currently utilised as the Government Hamidia Girls' School. The primary materials used for construction were brick, stone, and lime mortar. However, due to the lack of government protection and unsympathetic extensions, the structure's preservation has suffered, leaving it in a poor state. Indian National Trust for Art and Cultural Heritage (INTACH), Bhopal Chapter is currently working on its conservation.

Hamidia Hospital, constructed in the 1920s CE, is situated on Sultania Road, near the Royal Market. Initially known as Prince of Wales Hospital until 1937–38 CE, it was later renamed as Hamidia Hospital. The building was commissioned during the reign of Sultan Jahan Begum and features a clock tower. The hospital showcases various architectural elements, such as jharokhas (balconies), pavilions, moulded plinth stones, decorative stone stairs, semi-circular arches, ventilators, and decorative pillars. The entire structure is visually striking due to its construction using red sandstone, lending it a distinct reddish hue. With a high plinth of 2 metres, the hospital exhibits a character and style akin to the central library. Despite being an unprotected monument, the hospital is owned by the state government and has been well-preserved. Presently, it houses the blood bank of Hamidia Hospital.

The school exemplifies a blend of Mughal and Colonial architecture, having been constructed in the 1830s CE. Its rectangular design incorporates two internal courtyards. The front facade showcases intricately carved floral patterns on its arched openings and domes. Inside, the front foyer features lime plaster arch niches adorned with carvings. Additionally, the facade is embellished with carved brackets, a leaf motif cornice, and ornamental windows, as attested by local residents. The interior of the building also boasts arched doors with carved wooden panels and frames (chowkhats). Arched niches on the walls further exemplify the influence of Mughal architecture. The parapet wall exhibits carved patterns, and in certain areas, interior balusters are integrated into the parapet wall. As a load-bearing structure made of bricks and stones, the building incorporates wooden beams, stone ceilings, and brick vaulted ceilings. Some of the original wooden doors and windows with intricate carvings have survived in various locations, preserving their historic integrity.

According to local history shared by Shri Rizwan Uddin Ansari, who administers the Facebook page Bhopali Tales, the Sulemania Middle School near Moti Masjid in Bhopal has an interesting past. Originally constructed in the 1830s CE, it served as the residence of Phool Begum, the wife of Amir Mohammad Khan and the mother of Nawab Jehangir Mohammad Khan. Later, during the rule of Sikander Begum between 1850 and 1860 CE, it became the residence of Chief Minister Jamal Uddin Khan. Subsequently, from the 1870s to the 1890s CE, the building was used as a Taksal, a place for coin minting. Finally, in the early 1900s CE, during the reign of Sultan Jahan Begum, a girls' college named after her sister, Suleman Jehan Begum, was established near Moti Masjid, and this building was converted into a school known as Phool Mahal school. Following Sultan Jahan Begum's passing, the names of the schools were swapped, and since then, the Phool Mahal School has been referred to as Sulemania School. For the past century, the building has been operating as a school.[130]

The building, constructed in the second quarter of the nineteenth century, showcases a typical architectural style of that era, blending both colonial and Islamic influences. Its front facade features steps leading to an Islamic-style adaptation of a colonial entrance hall with an Islamic finial at the top, exemplifying the fusion of these architectural elements. Additionally, pavilions with domical roofs are located at the end of colonial-style verandas, adorned with Islamic parapets and double circular colonial columns, further reflecting the mix of architectural styles. The building is symmetrical along two axes and boasts a double-height centre hall with jack arch roofing.

Originally serving as a library, the building underwent a transformation into the office of the Lokayukta, following the enactment of the Lokayukta Act in 1981 CE. It was previously known as the Hamidia Library and had served as the first Vidhan Sabha during the Commissioner's period in Bhopal. Today, the office of the Lokayukta is located in this historic structure. Built using stone and brick, the building remains in a good state of preservation, though it has undergone renovations in recent years.[131]

The Imperial Bank, situated in ShahJehanabad, began its construction on 21st December 1921 CE under the reign of Nawab Sultan Jahan Begum. Displaying colonial influences, the building features a simple exterior design with circular columns on a square base. The entrance portico boasts semicircular openings, while ornate stone grills adorn the parapet of the structure. Within the same compound, one can find a platform that likely served as a stage, as well as two graves crafted from carved sandstone, topped with chatri-like structures. Additionally, the compound encompasses five small houses with sloping roofs adorned with terracotta tiles.

Putli Ghar, established in 1902 CE, is situated in close proximity to Bara Bagh. Initially, it served as the chimney for a combined ginning mill, saw mill, grass press, and a flour mill. Notably, during its time, it held the distinction of being the tallest chimney in the state. The ground level housed a boiler, and the factory had provisions for electricity production. On the exterior, a spiral staircase is visible, adding to its distinctive appearance. Constructed using brick and lime mortar, the structure showcases exposed brickwork. The name "Putli Ghar" derived from the continuous jumping of cotton seeds, which occurred during the process of separating them from cotton in the ginning process.[132]

Hayat Afza Bagh was built by Nawab Sultan Jahan Begum during her time as the heir apparent. From the 1950s CE, the grounds have been utilised for the Post Graduate Basic Training (PGBT) College, and since the 1980s CE, Geetanjali College has also operated from here.

Originally, the place was designed as a char bagh, featuring an arrangement of fruit and other trees. A significant reservoir, deep and continuously filled with water, was constructed in the area. The structure that covers the tank is so large that it gives the appearance of a palace. Inside, there is a spacious hall surrounded by corridors and rooms on all sides. Additionally, there are covered verandas at the front and an entrance vestibule. The building boasts a flat roof.[133]

Interestingly, due to the water storage below the structure, the interiors are naturally ventilated with cool air, along with an efficient water system. It is believed that during the Nawabi era, this place might have been used for entertainment and recreation. Currently, the maintenance of Hayat Afza Bagh is handled by the Public Works Department (PWD). However, it lacks formal protection as an official monument.

Minto Hall has a significant history and architecture. It was commissioned by Nawab Sultan Jahan Begum during the early 20th century CE. The hall was intended to serve as a Durbar Hall for receiving and entertaining exclusive guests, with the foundation stone laid on November 12, 1909 CE, by Lord Earl Minto, the viceroy of India, and Lady Minto. The naming of Minto Hall after Lord and Lady Minto was a tribute to their visit to Bhopal, signifying the special connection between the Nawab and the British Empire. However, they never visited the structure. Despite its initial purpose as a Durbar Hall, it was never utilised for commencing durbars during Sultan Jahan Begum's reign. It underwent changes in patronage during its construction from Nawab Sultan Jahan Begum to her son, Nawab Hamidullah Khan.

Minto Hall showcases an Indo-colonial architectural style, skillfully merging British Colonial and provincial Nawabi elements. The building features a rectilinear plan with a two-storey Colonial Durbar Hall at its centre, flanked by arcade aisles and ancillary rooms on both sides. A continuous colonnade verandah, adorned with paired Doric columns, encircles the structure, providing access from four cardinal directions through four entrances. Eight staircase towers grace the building, enhancing its grandeur. The exteriors boast white facades accentuated by red-painted towers, complemented by pediments, ornate brackets, cornices, decorative mouldings, and urns. Inside, the walls and ceilings are adorned with lavish floral ornamentation,

Minto Hall

showcasing a harmonious blend of colonial and Nawabi architectural aesthetics. The building's northern terrace offers a picturesque view of the Lower Lake and the skyline of Old Bhopal. Notably, Minto Hall's elevation symbolically mirrors the imperial crown of India, a tribute to King George V, Emperor of India.

Over time, Minto Hall transformed its usage and functions. It served as the headquarters for the princely state's army, a financial advisory office under the British, and a skating facility for the royal family. In 1946 CE, it became the 'Inter-College,' later known as 'Hamidia College,' marking the foundation of higher education in the state. Eventually, on September 9, 1956 CE, Minto Hall became

the Legislative Assembly (Vidhan Sabha) of Madhya Pradesh, playing a crucial role in the state's governance until the inauguration of a new assembly building on August 3, 1996 CE.

The construction of Minto Hall was driven by Sultan Jahan Begum's desire for progress and the expression of her individuality through various reforms and buildings, including her own walled mini-city called Ahmedabad and palaces like Qaser-e-Sultani. Understanding the context of Minto Hall's construction and its cultural significance requires exploring the socio-cultural context during the rule of its three main patrons: Nawab Sultan Jahan Begum, Nawab Hamidullah Khan, and the state government of Madhya Pradesh.[134]

Edward Museum (Central Library)

The Central Library, originally known as the Edward Museum, was constructed in 1908 CE and is situated near the railway station. Initially, the building served as an exhibition space to showcase the royal amenities.

The architecture of the Central Library is a captivating blend of Islamic and colonial styles. Made predominantly of red sandstone, the entrance features a porch adorned with slender ornamental veins, decorative merlons, and jharokhas projecting on the sides. At the heart of the building is a spacious hall with a high ceiling, illuminated by skylights from above. Distinct colonial influences are evident in the ventilators near the ceiling, which operate using ropes, and the gallery that encircles the first floor.

Constructed with dressed stone and showcasing pointed arches, the building boasts octagonal bastion-like towers at each of its four corners, culminating in Chhatris with domes. Additionally, smaller Chhatris grace the four corners of the inner square of the raised roof above the central hall. The building is surrounded by a battlement-designed parapet, while stone jalis elegantly cover the windows. The primary construction materials used are stone and mortar, and the well-preserved Central Library is currently under government ownership.

General Obaidullah, the second son of Sultan Jahan Begum, played a crucial role in establishing a Yacht Club along the shores of the upper lake. However, at present, only remnants of the club's existence can be observed.

NAWAB HAMIDULLAH KHAN (1926-1960 CE)

His full name was Nawab Sikandar Saulat Iftikhar-Ul-Mulk Bahadur Hamidullah Khan. He was the 3rd and last, and the only son who survived Begum Sultan Jahan, ascending the throne on 9th June 1926 CE.

Nawab Hamidullah Khan attended the Mohammedan Anglo-Oriental College (MAO College), now the Aligarh Muslim University, graduating in 1905 CE, and the Allahabad University, graduating with a BA in Law in 1915 CE.[135]

On 5th September 1925 CE, at Peshawar, Nawab Hamidullah Khan married Maimoona Sultan Shah Banu Begum Sahiba (1900–1982 CE), the great-great-granddaughter of Padshah Shuja Shah Durrani of Afghanistan. The couple had three daughters: Abida Sultan Begum Sahiba, Nawab Mehr-i-Taj Sajida Sultan Begum Sahiba, and Rabia Sultan Begum Sahiba (1916–2001 CE). He married a second time in 1947 CE. This time to Aftab Jahan Begum Sahiba (1919–2002 CE), the daughter of a local Muslim family from Bhopal. The couple had one daughter, Farzana Begum Sahiba (1948 CE). He remained the Chancellor of Aligarh Muslim University from September 1930 to April 1935 CE.[136]

He, too, had a Hindu Prime Minister in Raja Awadh Narayan Bisariya. He was the first male ruler of Bhopal in five generations. Prior to becoming the Nawab, he was appointed Chief Secretary to his mother's government. He was an able administrator and politician. Though he headed the rather small state of Bhopal, he was politically very adroit. Thus, he was appointed Chancellor of the prestigious Chamber of Princes on two occasions. At the 2nd Round Table

Noor-Us-Sabah

Conference, he advocated the independence of India in his capacity as Chancellor of the Chamber of Princes. This action of his was praised by Gandhiji. Hamidullah developed a very good administrative system. The Municipal Corporation Ordinance was promulgated during his tenure. Even the Queen of England was full of praise for this system. He had a lot of concern for his subjects. In 1942 CE, bad weather had a severe effect on standing crops, and Nawab Hamidullah promptly took steps to alleviate the suffering of his people. Dussehra and Eid-Ul-Fitr were the only festivals officially celebrated in the state of Bhopal during his tenure. He donated land for the construction of the prestigious Cricket Club of India (CCI) in Mumbai. In addition, he also donated land for the Jamia Millia Islamia in New Delhi.

The New Vihar at Sanchi was built by him. The inauguration ceremony of the Vihar saw the arrival of many distinguished guests, both Indian and foreign: Dr. Rajendra Prasad, Dr. S. Radhakrishnan,

and Pt. J. L. Nehru. Prime Minister of Japan Mr. Unu, the Prime Minister of Burma, to name some of them. The Nawab had severe problems walking and therefore, thus, he went by helicopter to the site.[137]

Nawab Hamidullah started the Hamidia Inter College at Minto Hall in Bhopal. To begin with, it was affiliated with the Ajmer Education Board. He introduced cycle polo in Bhopal. He was a very good shooter and an ace pilot. In typical erstwhile royal style, he was a keen golfer too. On the death of his Prime Minister, the palace that Hamidullah had gifted him was taken over by the government of Madhya Pradesh, and it housed the office of the R.T.O. for many years after the state was formed.[138]

Chiklod Kothi

During the reign of Nawab Hamidullah Khan, Sultan Jahan Begum oversaw the construction of the Noor-us-Sabah. This magnificent building was intended as the residence for the heir apparent, Nawab Abida Sultan, and also served as the chief secretary Sarfi Khas's abode. With a picturesque view of the lake, the Noor-us-Sabah featured a baradari and a small swimming tank.

Nawab Shahriyar Mohammad Khan, the son of Nawab Abida Sultan, learned to swim here under the guidance of an expert brought in from Bombay, who was paid a handsomely for his services.

Today, the Noor-us-Sabah palace has been transformed into a hotel and has undergone elaborate extensions to cater to modern-day hospitality requirements. The architectural features of the building include large circular pillars, high ceilings, and ornate cornices, adding to its allure. While the palace is currently under private ownership and has been preserved remarkably well, the new additions have altered its original character. Despite the changes, the Noor-us-Sabah continues

to captivate with its historical significance and grandeur.

Chiklod Kothi was a picturesque hunting resort (and later a popular picnic spot) that once belonged to Nawab Hamidullah Khan. When Pt. Jawaharlal Nehru visited Bhopal in 1946 CE, just a year before India's Independence, the Nawab extended his hospitality by arranging a lunch for him with the members of Bhopal Rajya Praja Mandal at the Chiklod Kothi.

During this meeting, Nehru expressed that Independence was on the verge of being a reality, and it was crucial to focus on educational initiatives across the nation. In response, the Nawab, agreeing with

Nehru's views, established the Hamidia Inter College at the Minto Hall, incredibly, within just three days.

The Cambridge School holds the distinction of being the oldest and first English medium school in Bhopal. It was founded during the reign of Nawab Hamidullah Khan, in 1932 CE.

Throughout its existence, the school earned a reputation as one of the finest educational institutions in the city. Its establishment marked a significant milestone in the promotion of English medium education in the region. As of today, the Cambridge School is under the administration of the state government. The school caters to students from nursery to the twelfth grade.

In the heart of Bhopal, where once the streets of Ibrahimpura, Chowk, and Loha Bazar bustled with activity, a transformation took place under the patronage of Nawab Hamidullah Khan. In front of Kala Darwaza, he constructed a row of twelve shops known as the "Royal Market". The motivation behind this ambitious endeavour was to cater to the immediate needs of the Nawab's family, who often had to procure goods from Bombay and foreign lands. Once a week, a special day was designated by Nawab Hamidullah for his family's shopping. On this day, the shops were lavishly decorated, and security was bolstered to ensure the safety and comfort of the royals, including red carpets being rolled out on the roads leading to the market.

Among the esteemed establishments within the Royal Market, Bombay Stores held a prominent place. Owned by Abdul Hafeez Khan, also known as Nawab Miyan, this departmental store offered a selection of high-quality products curated according to the preferences of the royal family. Another renowned store was Madan Lal and Brothers, owned by Madan Lal and his brother Laxmi Narayan, who were celebrated jauharis (jewellers) of the Bhopal State. Their jewellery shop in Royal Market showcased an array of regal jewellery.

Apart from these establishments, other notable shops graced Royal Market, such as Lal Sahab Ki Dukaan, which catered to various needs of imported motor parts, Industrial Sports for sporting goods, tailoring shops for custom-made garments, Chicory restaurant to satisfy culinary cravings, and Bright Clean Laundry to keep the royals' attire pristine. Royal Market lost its glory after the Nawabs' era. Now, it's mostly occupied by chemist shops and pathology labs due to the nearby development of Gandhi Medical College.[139]

Nawab Hamidullah Khan commissioned the construction of the Sophia Masjid, which takes architectural inspiration from France. The mosque's design is reminiscent of the renowned Jama Mosque in Paris, showcasing a captivating fusion of Islamic and art deco architectural styles. Notably, the Sofia Mosque features a distinctive single minaret.

The mosque boasts two hemispherical domes adorned with green tile terrazzo, serving as a striking crown. One of these domes houses the wazoo area of the mosque, featuring a central fountain that provides water for the devotees. These domes rest upon an octagonal upper wall adorned with art deco-style openings. The prayer hall is situated between the two domes, and it is supported by a single pillar arrangement.

Sophia Mosque exhibits intricate craftsmanship with its exquisite keyhole-shaped openings with circular-cut marble jalis. Additionally, the mosque is home to the cenotaphs of Sultan Jahan Begum and Nawab Hamidullah Khan, honouring their memory within its premises.

The Imperial Pavilion, located near the Ahmedabad Palace, and was originally constructed as a palace, exclusively built for hosting England's King Edward VIII during the reign of Nawab Hamidullah Khan in the early 20th century CE. The palace was a venue for tiger hunts, and its creation was entrusted to the renowned Italian architect, Heinz.

The architectural splendour, uniqueness and rarity of the design of the Imperial Pavilion lies in the symmetrical layout of the two identical buildings. High circular pillars of double height form the facade of the portico. Pointed arches, jaali work, and stucco work are some of the salient features of the building. It is built in a modern style, boasting of French windows and Italian marble. In 1960 CE, recognizing the palace's grandeur, it was converted into a hotel. At that time, it was acknowledged as one of the five most prestigious hotels in India, thus earning it a place in the esteemed World Guide of Hotels. The hotel occupies a sprawling 8-acre property, enveloped by expansive lawns and gardens. It stands atop a hill, offering a view of Bada Talab, while being surrounded by lush green forest-covered hills.

Imperial Sabre

Today, as the Imperial Sabre Hotel, it holds a rich historical background and boasts an impressive architectural design. The Imperial Sabre has played host to Mahatma Gandhi (in its former avatar as the Imperial Pavilion), Sardar Patel, Rajeev Gandhi, numerous kings, queens, and ministers from various states. With banquet facilities capable of accommodating up to 5,000 guests and ample car parking

space, the hotel is renowned as the premier venue for weddings in the city of Bhopal.[140]

15

THE BRITISH PROTECTORATE:

THE ROLE OF BRITISHERS IN THE BHOPAL STATE

Situated in central India, erstwhile Bhopal found itself strategically placed among larger princely states and regional powers. Recognizing the need for stability and protection. Bhopal's rulers forged agreements with the British, forming a significant protectorate that influenced the region. In this arrangement, Bhopal maintained nominal sovereignty while seeking British assistance and safeguarding. The historical ties between the British East India Company and the Bhopal State unfolded through intricate agreements and alliances, continuing to its subjection into the British Empire as a result of the Government of India Act 1858, as a princely state.

These agreements not only shielded Bhopal from threats by neighbouring states and external forces but also integrated it into broader colonial endeavours. The British Protectorate extended beyond defence to encompass diplomacy, economics, and governance.

In the late 18th century CE, the British sought to unify their Presidency Armies with an overland movement. On 23 February 1778 CE, led by Colonel Leslie, a force comprising of native infantry, artillery, cavalry, and Mughal horsemen from the Nawab of Oudh was to link Kalpi to the Bombay Presidency. However, disputes with Bundela Chiefs diverted Leslie's path. Colonel Thomas Goddard took over the command, leading the march through Bhilsa, Khemlasa, and Hoshangabad, crossing the river Narmada on 2 December 1778 CE.

The Nawab of Bhopal's spontaneous aid during this march held significant consequences. Despite dissidence amongst her subjects, the Nawab, guided by Mamola Bai, supported Goddard's forces, establishing goodwill that would impact the 1818 Treaty with the British.[141]

Bhopal experienced unrest due to conflicts with neighbours like Bhonsle and Scindias, the Maratha chieftains. A siege of Bhopal by Raghuji Bhonsle in 1812-13 CE compelled Bhopal Nawab to urgently seek British protection. Around 1809 CE, Wazir Muhammad's initial attempts to secure British Government assistance and mediation against the Mahrathas were fruitless. Faced with self-preservation, the Nawab formed an alliance with Pindari leaders. In 1812 CE, Scindia and Raghuji Bhonsla formed an alliance to crush him, and Bhopal faced a siege from their combined armies in 1813 CE. Wazir Muhammad successfully defended his territory for nine months, forcing the Mahrathas to retreat.

Meanwhile, Central Province faced an internal threat from the Pindari menace. Recognizing the value of amicable Princes for security and rebellion suppression, the British aligned itself with Bhopal State's treaty negotiations to establish local garrisons against the Pindaris. Scindia aimed to renew the Bhopal siege the following year, but British interference, motivated by doubts about Bhonsla's loyalty and valuing Bhopal's role against the Pindaris, curtailed his efforts. However, Wazir Muhammad's connection with the British Government lacked formal engagement during his lifetime. Wazir Muhammad's passing in 1816 CE led to his second son, Nazar Muhammad ascending to the throne. Amid the onset of the Pindari war in 1817 CE, the British Government swiftly formed a close alliance with Bhopal. Pindari leaders had long sought refuge in Bhopal, aiding Nawabs against Scindia and Nagpur's attacks. Nazar Muhammad was displeased with this association and embraced the British alliance.

A mutual agreement was established, with terms suggested by Nazar Muhammad himself, alongside a pledge to offer his troops for British service. Although no formal treaty was penned, the exchanged correspondence on 13 October 1817 CE, held the significance and impact of a treaty. These terms were faithfully honoured, serving as the foundation for a subsequent formal treaty of perpetual friendship and alliance-the Treaty of Raisen. The Treaty guaranteed the state, required Bhopal to furnish 600 horse-borne cavalry and a 400 strong infantry, and was rewarded it with five districts in Malwa, and also the maintenance of the contingent. This grant included a provision for 6,000 rupees annual payment from district revenues to Khande Rao, the former manager. The guarantee was sealed by the British Government, culminating in the issuance of the 1818 sanad to Khande Rao by Nawab Nazar Muhammad, backed by Captain Stewart and later endorsed by Sir John Malcolm. The series of successive treaties continued until the state was eventually integrated into the Union of India following its attainment of independence.

During the colonial era of British rule in India, the territories were divided into two distinct categories: British India and the native Princely States. The hierarchical structure was outlined by the British Parliament in the Interpretation Act of 1889, defining "British India" as the regions within Her Majesty's dominions governed either directly by the Governor-General of India or by subordinate officers under the Governor-General's jurisdiction. This construct also extended to the broader term "India", encompassing British India and the territories of native princes or chiefs under the suzerainty of Her Majesty, ultimately overseen by the Governor-General and officers within the British India administration.

The sway of the British Crown over the 175 preeminent Princely States, which held considerable significance, was exercised through the central government of British India under the Viceroy. An additional 400, approximately, states were influenced by Agents who were accountable to the provincial governments of British India, led by a governor, lieutenant-governor, or chief commissioner. The distinction between "dominion" and "suzerainty" was most evident in the legal jurisdiction: the laws governing British India were based on British Parliament's legislation, enforced by the authorities of British India's different levels of governance, whereas the courts in the princely states operated under the rulers' authority.

The administrative landscape comprised presidencies, provinces, residencies, agencies, and princely states. Presidencies like Madras, Bombay, and Calcutta evolved into larger territories. Provinces were established under the British Crown, each with a legislative council and an administrative head. Residencies involved British Residents managing relations with princely states. Agencies were responsible for groups of princely states, led by British Agents. Princely states operated semi-autonomously, recognizing British authority in certain specific areas.

The Residencies of British India were political offices overseen by British Residents who managed relations between the Government of India and groups of princely states. The system emerged from subsidiary alliances after the Battle of Plassey, securing Bengal through deployment of troops and British Residents in Native States. The Resident advised on governance, intervened in succession, and symbolised suzerain relations.

The gun salute system determined rulers' precedence based on number of guns fired. Salute states held 3 to 21 gun salutes, signifying prestige. After independence, the Nizam of Hyderabad was replaced by the Maharana of Udaipur. The Privy Purse supported rulers until its abolition in 1971 CE. The rulers who were entitled to the highest 21-gun salute included the Nizam of Hyderabad, Maharaja of Mysore, and others.

The British intervention in the governance of the Bhopal state, despite the treaty's designation as a "perpetual friendship and alliance", was initiated as Bhopal fell under British protection. This intervention led to the establishment of a structured hierarchy of British officials, a reflection of arrangements seen in other princely states like Bikaner and Jodhpur, which had agreed to British oversight. Similarly, within Bhopal, a Political Agent held a prominent position, acting under the jurisdiction of the Governor General. This agent's responsibility was to provide reports to the "Agent to the Governor General" at the Central India Agency, with its headquarters situated in Indore. Notably, the Political Agent did not reside in the capital of the Bhopal State; instead, their headquarters were located in a cantonment at Sehore.

The Bhopal state fell under the Central India Presidency with a bunch of other Residencies and Agencies. The agency was a political unit comprising various princely states, having a political agent appointed for each state, whereas the residency. The central India agency consisted of various residencies and agencies. One such agency was Bhopal Agency that consisted of both salute and non-salute states. Bhopal, Narsinghgarh, Rajgarh and Khilchipur were salute states whereas Basoda, Kurwai, Maksudangarh, Mohammadgarh and Pathari were none-salute states. Bhopal Rulers held the title of Nawab and were awarded with the Hereditary Salute of 19 guns (21 guns locally).

Prior to this, Nawab Sikandar Begum had been actively consolidating her army in Bhopal after a commitment in the Raisen Treaty. Recognizing the need for a disciplined and well-trained force, she reorganised the Bhopal Army. The infusion of structure and professionalism marked a departure from the previous undifferentiated system. She modernised the funding model, moving away from reliance on Jagirdars, and instead began paying regular salaries from the treasury. Noteworthy changes included the establishment of a dedicated Artillery- the "Topkhana", and a revitalised Cavalry. Proper cantonments were set up, and a separate arsenal was constructed, symbolising the modernization of Bhopal's military apparatus. This period also witnessed Sikandar Begum's keen attention to soldier welfare, with regular reviews of military parades and provisions for the well-being of the soldiers.

Despite many reforms, the rebellion among Bhopal troops during the Mutiny of 1857 CE was a complex outcome driven by a convergence of various factors. Economic grievances formed a core catalyst, with soldiers frustrated by delayed salaries and the imposition of the "Zar-i-lain" tax, designed for barracks construction and maintenance. Moreover, the introduction of cartridges coated with animal fat that conflicted with religious beliefs acted as a potent symbol of British insensitivity. The troops' exposure to the broader Indian rebellion and leaders advocating united resistance played a role in their decision to revolt. Coupled with this was the underlying discontent with British interference in religious and cultural matters.

Maulvis of Bhopal actively supported the rebellion by preaching and advocating for "Jihad" against the British. For instance, the Maulvi of Masjid-e-Mankashah issued a "Fatwa" urging citizens to join and support the movement against the British. These religious figures played a role in propagating anti-British sentiments and rallying support for the rebellion. Similarly, Qudsia Begum, once favouring British intervention, experienced a shift. She embraced the mutiny's anti-British sentiment, likely driven by her waning authority and marginalisation, amplifying the rebellion's fervour in Bhopal.

The trajectory of Bhopal's response to the rebellion was shaped by this foundation of administrative foresight. As the rumblings of the Indian Mutiny reached Bhopal, Sikandar Begum's proactive stance became evident. She deftly managed to address the concerns of the sepoys within her jurisdiction. Amidst the broader rebellion, she acted to prevent internal divisions by curbing the spread of seditious pamphlets and messages, while maintaining open channels of communication with her military personnel.

Nawab Umrao Dulha played a crucial role in quelling the rebellion within Bhopal troops. Recognizing the urgency of the situation, he engaged directly with the discontented sepoys, utilising his influence and rapport to pacify their grievances. His measured approach and assurance of fair consideration for their demands resonated with the sepoys, helping to prevent further escalation of the rebellion. Moreover, Nawab Sikandar Begum's personal meeting with the sepoys at the Parade Ground was a masterstroke in addressing their concerns. Her immediate payment of their dues, demonstrated her commitment to their welfare and garnered their trust.

Notably, Sikandar Begum's measured approach extended to seeking the safety of British officers stationed in nearby Sehore cantonment, neutralising a potential point of conflict. Her strategic thinking became evident as she used loyal Afghan troops to guard the British contingent in Hoshangabad, creating a buffer against any aggressive moves by the mutineers. Nawab Sikandar Begum's adept handling of the Mutiny positively influenced British-Bhopal relations. Her prompt suppression of rebel elements and assurance of British officers' safety demonstrated loyalty to the British Crown and alignment with their interests. Collaborative actions, such as securing British agreement on succession terms for her daughter and maintaining a disciplined Bhopal Army, portrayed Bhopal as a stable and reliable ally.

In a gesture of gratitude for quelling the 1857 CE uprising, Lord Canning, the viceroy, conducted a durbar (court) on January 7, 1861 CE, in Jabalpur. The nawab received a special invitation, and the begum was bestowed a 'sanad', granting her the Pargana of Berasia, previously under the jurisdiction of Dhar state. This was a token of appreciation for her devoted services during the uprising. Addressing the Nawab, Lord Canning stated:[142]

"Sikander Begum! Your Highness is very welcome to the Durbar. I have long desired to thank you for the services which you have rendered to the queen's Government. Your Highness is the ruler of a state which is conspicuous in the history for never having been in arms against the british power and lately, when the state was beset and threatened by our enemies, you, a women, guided its affairs with courage, and ability and a success, that would have done honour to any statesman or soldier.....such services must not go unrewarded.
I now place in your hands, the grant in sovereignty of the district of Berasia. This district was formerly a dependency of the state of Dhar, but Dhar has, by rebellion, forfeited all claims to it; and it is now given in perpetuity to Bhopal for memorial of loyalty, under your wise and brave guidance in the time of trial....."[143]

In November of that year, she received the Grand Cross of the Star of India (GCSI) in Allahabad Durbar. As the sole female ruler, she captured the attention of all in attendance during these courts. During the Allahabad Durbar, the declaration was made that Bhopal would be granted a 19-gun salute. Among the 561 Princely states in British India, merely two were authorised for a 21-gun salute, while 17 states were granted a 19-gun salute – and Bhopal was counted among these.

In 1872 CE, Nawab ShahJehan Begum was honoured with the title of Grand Commander Star of India (GCSI). In 1877 CE, the nawab participated in the imperial gathering in Delhi, where she was presented with the banner and the medal.[144] By 1903 CE, the Imperial Service Troops had garnered a commendable reputation due to their remarkable display in the Honor Guard during the Delhi Durbar.[145] The Bhopal (Victoria) Lancers actively engaged in the review of His Majesty's Durbar held in Delhi in 1911 CE. As each squadron of the Lancers rode past in perfect synchronisation, they were met with enthusiastic cheers. His Majesty The King Emperor expressed his satisfaction with their brave performance, recalling his previous inspection of the regiment in Indore back in 1905 CE.[146]

In a memorandum dated August 12, 1817 CE, Thomas Munro addressed Lord Hastings, articulating, *"The strength of the British Government enables it to put down every rebellion, to repel every foreign invasion and to give its subjects a degree of protection which those of no native powers enjoy. Its laws and institutions also afford them a security from domestic operation, unknown in those States; but these advantages are dearly bought. They are purchased by the sacrifice of independence of national character and whatever renders a people respectable."*

D A Low identifies the Indian states—focusing particularly on the era following Queen Victoria's proclamation in 1858 CE, when interference in the internal affairs of states was ostensibly curtailed, in theory, to rectifying exceptional transgressions. However, as Copland's research illustrates concerning western India, such internal interventions occurred more frequently during certain periods than abstract policy would imply.

Despite the loyalty of the Bhopal nawabs, this did not lead to a reduction in British interference in both the state's internal affairs and the personal lives of the royalty. Historical records are replete with instances illustrating how Bhopal rulers were bound to seek discussions and permissions even for seemingly trivial state matters, along with personal issues like marital decisions. Each action's execution necessitated explicit approval from British authorities, essentially mandating their endorsement for any undertaken matter.

In her work "Hayat-e-ShahJehani," Begum Sultan vividly recounts instances where British authorities were required to grant permissions for both marriages of Nawab Shahjehan.[147] Another instance is a letter penned on May 20th, 1913 CE, by Nawab Hamidullah addressed to the Political Agent in Bhopal exemplifies the extent of British involvement. The letter seeks counsel from the Agent regarding the imposition of restrictions on alcohol consumption in the Darbar hall for guests, underscoring the meticulous scrutiny even over the minutest of matters in consultation with British authorities.[148]

The interaction between Bhopal and the British transcended political and administrative boundaries, encompassing deep personal connections. One striking example is the enduring friendship between an Indian ruler and the wife of a British Army officer. Colonel George Patrick Ranken, stationed in Bhopal in the early 20th century CE, and his wife Ada formed a remarkable bond with Nawab Sultan Jahan Begum.

Their acquaintance began when Ada Ranken and Sultan Jahan Begum were introduced at a garden party in 1904-05 CE. Despite Begum's Purdah practices, Ada was allowed into her tent.

Over the next few years, Ada and the Begum met on several occasions, and their friendship deepened. Even after Ada returned to England, their correspondence continued, marked by 22 surviving letters from Sultan Jahan Begum.

These letters, addressed primarily to Ada but also to her husband and daughter, delved into news from Bhopal, the Begum's family, shared friends, and fond recollections of their time together in India. Despite Begum's demanding role as the ruler of a substantial state, she made time to correspond with Ada, showing the depth of their bond. In one letter, she described the bustling preparations for a Viceregal visit to Bhopal in 1909 CE.

The final letter, dated 25 December 1929 CE, conveyed the Begum's condolences on the passing of Ada's sister, showing the sincere affection they held for each other's families. The Ranken Papers, a collection that includes these letters, drafts of Ada's article about Sultan Jahan Begum, photographs, Christmas cards, and Ada's drawing of the Begum, stand as a testament to the profound and enduring personal relationships that intertwined British individuals with Bhopal's ruling figures, going beyond the realm of politics and administration.

Nevertheless, this alliance bestowed a sense of stability upon the state, fostering both economic prosperity and cultural advancement. Paradoxically, while the rest of the Indian subcontinent was grappling with upheaval and financial depletion, the period marked a time of flourishing for the Bhopal state. The architectural opulence that emerged during this epoch stands as a testament to the multifaceted growth - economic, social, and cultural - achieved.

The British vested interest in enhancing connectivity between remote hinterlands and ports, facilitating the transport of raw materials to Britain. In this context, Bhopal, enjoying a safeguarded status, was also anticipated to contribute to this cause. An agreement was signed.[149] Consequently, the Bhopal Begums extended substantial contributions from both the state's coffers and their privy purse.[150] As a result, Bhopal evolved into a strategically positioned railway hub, intricately connected to the cardinal points of the north-south and east-west railway lines.

Bhopal's strong affiliations with the British also played a pivotal role in the introduction of English education within the region. The inception of the Cambridge School marked the establishment of the first English medium school in Bhopal. Moreover, the British influence distinctly manifests itself in the architectural legacy of Bhopal. Following the British protectorate, Bhopal's architectural landscape seamlessly incorporated colonial elements and British architectural methodologies and designs. This influence is evident across a substantial number of edifices constructed subsequent to the formal integration of British governance with the Bhopal Nawabs' administration.

These cumulative advancements, primarily underscored by a robust infrastructural framework and strategic geographic location, paved the trajectory for Bhopal's designation as a state capital post-independence. The Nawabi architectural infrastructure readily provided the requisite spaces for administrative and legislative activities to unfold.

THE GROWTH AND DEVELOPMENT OF BHOPAL

The city of Bhopal, often perceived as a modern settlement, reveals itself to be a comparatively ancient town upon closer examination of its history. This essay delves into the multifaceted layers of Bhopal's growth and development, offering insights into its chronological evolution and the patterns that have shaped its unique character. A fascinating journey through its historical phases unravels the city's transformation from a natural terrain to its current state.

Bhopal's story is one of adaptation and progression, with each era leaving its indelible mark on the city's landscape. From its early foundations associated with Raja Bhoj to the reigns of the Nawabs and modern leaders,

Bhopal's development journey showcases a dynamic blend of cultural heritage, architectural wonders, and urban planning. Furthermore, the city's journey through time reveals shifts in its expansion pattern.

Bhopal, a city located on a hilly terrain, exhibits distinctive geographical features characterised by sloping landscapes towards the north and southeast. These slopes are adorned with hillocks of varying altitudes, prominently situated in the southwest and northwest sides of the city. Seven distinctive hillocks, along with their accompanying valleys, encompass the entirety of Bhopal. These hills include Neori hills, Idgah hills, Shamla hills, Arera hills, Kaliyasot hills, Kerwa hills, and Katara hills.

The city is positioned upon a stratum of red sandstone situated on the Malwa Plateau, encompassed by a diverse array of hillocks within and surrounding its environs. The uppermost layers of these hillocks and their accompanying slopes predominantly consist of hard soil intermixed with boulders. Additionally, black cotton soil is discernible at various depths, commencing at 1.25 metres in the northeastern sector, while the hinterland areas contain deposits of sand, stone, black basalt, and morum, which serve as viable building materials.

Bhopal due to its abundant forest cover and water bodies enjoys a moderate climate, with temperature fluctuations spanning from 50 degrees Fahrenheit to 104 degrees Fahrenheit (approximately 10 degree Celsius to 40 degree Celsius).

Natural drainage within the city is primarily facilitated by three main streams, complemented by a network of small nallahs and rivelets. In the northeastern precincts, the river Halali serves as a crucial drainage outlet, while the southeastern side is supported by the Kaliasot river. Both these watercourses eventually merge with the Betwa River, with Halali doing so near Vidisha and Kaliasot in proximity to Bhojpur. Conversely, in the southwestern quadrant of the city, the drainage system is primarily managed by an assortment of small nallahs, which converge and discharge into the Kolar river, ultimately joining the mighty Narmada River.

The prehistoric phase in Bhopal's development marks the earliest evidence of human occupation in the city's natural terrain. A number of archaeological sites, boasting artwork dating back to the Paleolithic and Mesolithic eras are evidence of human occupation in these regions. This era witnessed the artistic expressions of early inhabitants, giving us a glimpse into their lives and surroundings.

Beyond Bhimbetka, Bhopal conceals numerous other archaeological sites rich in prehistoric rock art. Sporadic rock art is found in the premises of Indira Gandhi Rastriya Manav Sangrahalaya (IGRMS), Maulana Azad National Institute of Technology (MANIT) cwampus, Jhiri Village, ManuabhanTekri and Reechan Kho. These sites harbour exquisite paintings within its caves, offering a unique perspective. These artworks, set against the backdrop of the Vindhyachal range, mirror the productive and harmonious existence of the ancient people, depicting animal figures such as buffalo and deer. The rock art here unveils the lives of pastoral communities, hunters, and gatherers, portraying rituals, cultural identities, and pastoral concerns of the time. Jawra houses a towering 14-foot-tall animal painting that exemplifies the wealth of prehistoric records in this region. Dr. Narayan Vyas, retired Superintending Archaeologist (ASI), says to The Times of India in an interview, "Around five or six years ago, a lot of stone tools were found in this place (Reechan Kho), and a lot of things are yet to be discovered as well. The paintings here exhibit the life of people – the way they dressed, etc – and how the animals were of that time. A lot of daily activities, like them working, cooking and performing other chores — are depicted,"[151] These evidence substantiate the presence of a pastoral population in the region prior to the introduction of agriculture and settled communities. It suggests that the contemporary city of Bhopal has evolved naturally from the historical progression of hunting-gathering nomadic groups transitioning into early settlers.

While the surrounding areas of Bhopal, such as Vidisha, Sanchi, and Raisen, basked in the grandeur of the Mauryan and Gupta Empires, evidenced by the architectural remnants and historical references found in various texts, Bhopal remained relatively obscure during that epoch. Nevertheless, it is conceivable that before evolving into the town of Bhojpal, the region might have harboured a diminutive village. The paucity of evidence pertaining to established settlements preceding the arrival of Raja Bhoj in this region, who instigated the construction of a lake around which a nascent town emerged, has led some scholars to postulate the existence of a small village before Raja

Bhoj's tenure.

The inception of both historical and architectural remnants can be traced back to Raja Bhoj's ambitious undertaking - the construction of a dam and the Bhojeshwar Shiva Temple, named after him, between 1010- 1055. Raja Bhoj's monumental Bhim Kund lake, earned its name due to its grandeur and expansive size. The name "Bhopal" finds its roots in the combination of "Bhoj" (referring to Raja Bhoj) and "Pal" (referring to the dam he constructed), thus giving rise to the appellation "Bhojpal." Over time, this name naturally evolved into "Bhopal."

Tradition also suggests that Raja Bhoj erected a fort near the lake upon which the present city stands, in addition to another fort near the Bhojeshwar temple located in Bhojpur. During this pivotal period, it is widely believed that a village or small town began to coalesce around the Bhim Kund lake. Simultaneously, another settlement took shape around the Bhojeshwar Temple, eventually becoming known as Bhojpur. Dost Muhammad Khan, upon his establishment of Bhopal State in 1722 CE, linked the newly built Fatehgarh Fort with the older fort in Bhojpal that was attributed to Raja Bhoja. On the other hand, the Bhojpur fort served as a prison until the rule of Begums in the nineteenth century.

Udyaditya, the grandson of Raja Bhoj, saw his wife Rani Shalmali undertake the construction of a Sabha Mandal near Raja Bhoj's fort, thereby expanding the city towards the northeast. This structure was believed to have been modelled after the Sabha Mandal in Dhar, which was the capital of the Paramara rulers. Historical records from the Nawabi era indicate that this Sabha Mandal stood at the location where the present Jama Masjid now stands.

According to a legend, Rani Shalmali is also believed to be credited with the construction of Swastik Nagar, a planned settlement designed in the shape of the sacred Hindu symbol, the swastika. However, as of now, there is no reported archaeological evidence to substantiate this claim.

Another legend suggests that during the reign of Qudsia Begum, two sects of Jainism, Shwetaber and Digamber, were in conflict over the ruins of a temple located in Sher-i-Khas. Qudsia Begum initiated the construction of the Jama Masjid at the very site and relocated the Jain sculptures to two separate temples, each built for one of the sects, in order to resolve the dispute. These two temples are still present in the Jama Masjid Chowk.

According to Luard, it is certain that there was never a significant or large town in this location during this phase. In simpler terms, this area did not host a substantial settlement or urban centre. While there might have been plans or intentions to establish a town in this area, or some initial efforts may have been made towards that end, the absence of a sizable town can be attributed to the declining influence or authority of the Parmara Chiefs during the successors of Udayaditya Parmara. This suggests that the rulers' warning control may have impeded further urban development of Bhojpal.

As the Parmaras' influence waned, the Gond Kingdom began to rise in this region. However, Bhopal, in particular, did not experience significant growth because it was not the capital city or a major town during the rule of the Gond Rulers. The Gond rulers governed from Ginnaurgarh. Consequently, Bhopal did not undergo any substantial expansion during this period. Towards the end of the Gond rule, Rani Kamlapati constructed a palace for herself in the year 1722 CE. This palace, known as the Kamalapati Palace, was situated on the old eastern dam of Raja Bhoja and existed at the centre of the settlement.

The initial and successful endeavour to transform Bhopal into a city was initiated by Dost Mohammad Khan. In the year 1722 CE, he embarked on the construction of Fatehgarh Fort. This decision was inspired by a dream he had during a hunting expedition in the nearby jungles of the region.

Dost Mohammad Khan not only laid the foundation of Fatehgarh Fort but also encompassed a substantial area with a robust defensive wall, effectively creating the space required for a city. He ingeniously connected this newly built fort with the pre-existing fort associated with Raja Bhoj by constructing a connecting wall. The area enclosed within these fortifications came to be known as Sehr-i-Khas or City Proper, marking the inception of Bhopal's development as a city. This visionary move by Dost Mohammad Khan was instrumental in shaping the city's future.

During the time of Nawab Yar Muhammad, the capital was situated in Islamnagar (now Jagdishpur), which resulted in Bhopal experiencing a lack of royal construction and city expansion efforts. Nevertheless, Mamola Bai, his wife, oversaw the construction of three mosques, all located at the southern end of Fatehgarh fort. These mosques were named after her: Masjid Maji Sahiba, Kalan and Retghat (both old and new), and another mosque named after Yar Mohammad's daughter, called Masjid Qudsia Begum. Consequently, it can be observed that during this phase, there was no expansion of the city's boundaries to include new areas, but rather, the construction efforts concentrated on intensifying the settlement within the existing limits.

However, this situation changed when Nawab Faiz Muhammad returned to Bhopal, making it the principal town. It was during the reign of Nawab Hayat Muhammad that significant enhancements were made to the city's defences and walls by his Dewan Chhote Khan. Chhote Khan also oversaw the construction of a dam to control the flow of water in the northeast direction, which led to the creation of another lake known as Chhota Talab or Pukhta Pul Talab, meaning the "Lake of the Stone Bridge." This development also contributed to the expansion of the outer city around Chhota Talab.

The fortification served to partition the city into two distinct tiers: one located within the protective confines of the fort wall, and the other situated outside these fortified walls. However, in the years 1812-13 CE, during an attack by forces from Nagpur and Gwalior, the entire town situated outside Dost Muhammad's protective wall was reduced to ruins. The process of recovery only began with the succession of Nazar Muhammad. Nevertheless, the times remained turbulent, and the houses constructed during this period were modest structures with thatched roofs.

Qudsia Begum, the wife of Nazar Mohammad, assumed the role of regent for Sikandar Begum following the accidental demise of Nazar Mohammad. During her regency, she embarked on several significant construction projects. Notably, she commissioned the construction of her own residential palace known as Gauhar Mahal, a grand mosque called Jama Masjid, and initiated the development of numerous water features and gardens in the vicinity of the city.

The primary focus of these construction endeavours was centred in and around Shehr-i-Khas, with the adjoining areas of the previous boundaries of Fatehgarh Fort. Meanwhile, her efforts in creating water works and gardens extended far beyond the city limits. Notable among these were Bada Bagh located to the north and Aish Bagh situated to the east of the existing settlement.

Throughout the reign of Qudsia Begum, the population of the city was primarily composed of Afghan adventurers who sought military service and had no intentions of establishing permanent settlements. However, during the tenure of Nawab Jehangir, significant efforts were made to address this situation. He encouraged people to settle permanently and engage in the construction of good houses.

As an initial measure, Nawab Jehangir relocated the troops, which had been a somewhat disruptive presence, outside the city limits to Jehangirabad, situated on the south-west of Chhota Talab. He also built a palace named Jehangirabad Kothi for his residence. This strategic move proved successful, and the city immediately began to transform into a flourishing trading hub. Jehangir's endeavour laid the foundation for the city's development as a permanent and prosperous centre for trade and commerce. Upon her succession, Sikander Begum prioritised the development of the army and forces, as per the commitments outlined in the Raisen Treaty. Additionally, she effectively quelled the rebellion of 1857 CE, a significant and time-consuming endeavour that left limited opportunities for infrastructure development. Nonetheless, Sikander Begum also supervised the construction of the Moti Masjid and the Moti Mahal.

Demonstrating her characteristic vigour, Sikandar Begum embarked on enhancing the city's infrastructure. Her efforts included the establishment of well-constructed roads and the installation of street lamps to illuminate the thoroughfares, enhancing the urban environment and improving the quality of life for the city's inhabitants. During this phase of development, settlement growth entailed the occupation of the area that lay between Shehr-i-Khas and Jehangirabad.

The zenith of infrastructural development in Bhopal was realised during the reign of ShahJehan Begum. She initiated the development and growth of an entirely new suburb, ShahJehanabad, taking inspiration from her father, Jehangir. This fortified suburb was notable for housing her monumental palace, known as the Taj Mahal, as well as the grand Taj-ul-Masajid mosque, which stood as a symbol of architectural magnificence during that era.

ShahJehanabad featured a distinctive three-tiered system of lakes that cleverly followed the natural slope of the land, descending from the upper to the lower levels. These lakes were individually named as Motia Talab, Noor Talab, and Hussain Bakshi ki Tallaiya. In conjunction with these beautiful lakes, ShahJehan Begum also oversaw the construction of Benazir Palace, intended for use as her summer residence. This emphasis on water and its incorporation into urban planning played a crucial role in the city's evolution and development.

The significance of water in Bhopal's history dates back to the early 11th century when Raja Bhoj created the upper lake. Subsequently, various rulers in different periods recognized the topographical advantage and established numerous additional lakes and water bodies. This concerted effort to harness and incorporate water resources earned Bhopal its well-deserved title as "The City of Lakes."

ShahJehan Begum's ambitious construction endeavours extended beyond the boundaries of her own suburb. Her projects encompassed the Idgah hills in the west, where she constructed the Idgah itself, and reached as far as Bagh Nishat Afza in the north. Her initiatives also extended eastward to the Bhopal Railway Junction, resulting in the expansion of the city towards the northern side of Bada Talab, significantly altering its urban landscape.

Following in the footsteps of her mother, ShahJehan, Sultan Jahan, upon ascending to power, initiated a similar path of development. She established her own suburb to the west of the city and constructed her residential palace, known as Ahmedabad Palace. This palace served as the centrepiece around which the Ahmedabad suburb gradually took shape. In addition to these endeavours, Sultan Jahan undertook the development of the Sultania Infantry, a unit meant for Imperial Service Troops. This initiative involved the renovation of areas within ShahJehanabad, eventually becoming known as Sultania Infantry Lines.

During her reign, Bhopal was surveyed by C. E. Luard, and he provided a comprehensive account of the city in his Gazetteer of Bhopal.[152] A somewhat unique account of the city's landscape is as follows:

"There are many large houses, often two and three stories high. These are as a rule enclosed by high walls and though often massive and well built add but little to the beauty of the town. Many of the streets, however, are by no means devoid of beauty, the irregularity of the houses' which form them, the sudden turns leading into unsuspected squares, and the great gateways which pierce the walls of bigger dwellings adding much to the picturesqueness. One most noticeable feature is the all prevailing sandstone dust, which covers everything, houses, trees and even the pariah dogs with a red pall. The houses are substantial, as the sandstone which abounds in the neighbourhood is the principal material used in building, even small houses being constructed of it."[153]

Hamidullah Khan, on the other hand, directed his efforts toward modernising and industrialising the city. Under his leadership, several industries were established, including a Cotton Mill and a Flour Mill. Furthermore, he acted upon the counsel of Jawaharlal Nehru and founded a Hamidia College, which found its initial home in Minto Hall. Notably, two of the city's most prominent palaces, Jehan Numa and Imperial Sabre, were also constructed during his tenure. These palaces have since earned a reputation as some of the finest hotels in the country.

It is noteworthy that during the era of the Nawabs, the city's development and expansion predominantly occurred in the northern vicinity of the Bada Talab. However, after India's independence, the city experienced substantial growth to the south of the lake, encompassing areas such as the BHEL Township, Polytechnic College, TT Nagar, MLA Bungalow Area, and more. This shift in the city's expansion reflects changes in urban planning and demographic patterns over time.

◇◇◇◇◇◇◇◇◇◇◇◇◇◇◇◇◇◇◇◇◇

APPENDICES

APPENDIX-1 : THE ORIGIN OF ORAKZAI PATHANS

The origins of the great Pathan warrior tribes that straddle today's Afghanistan and Pakistan's North-West Frontier are shrouded in a haze that merges legend into history. The Pathans date back to pre-Islamic times and are generally regarded as Aryans who moved eastwards from Arabia and Central Asia towards Persia and Afghanistan. Sir Olaf Caroe traces the origins of the Orakzai tribe to Karlane who was the fourth progenitor of the famous Pathan among tribes. The first three were all sons of Qais. The eldest. Sarbanr, was the ancestor of the Yusufzais, the Durranis, and the Tarins others. The second son, Bitan, headed Ghilzais, Lodis, and Suris whose dynasties ruled over northern India before the Moghuls. The third, Ghurghust, was the ancestor of Kakars and Jadoons. Karlanr was not one of Qais's sons (some say he was a son of Ghurghusht) but was a figurehead of the time whose tribal offspring included the Gorran, Orakzai, Afridi, Khattak, Masud, and Bangash.

The Orakzai were mainly Sunnis and settled in the Tirah Valley, which lies in Pakistan's tribal area. They moved from Persia to Afghanistan sometime in the seventh century. Each tribe was divided into clans-khels-who took their names after a family stalwart. Dost Mohammad Khan was an Orakzai who belonged to the Mirazi-khel. Other clans of the same tribe were the Jalal-khel of Lohari, with whom Dost initially stayed in India. It was from the Jalal-khel that Ahmad Khan (Sultan Doulah) was selected by Sikandar Begum, as her granddaughter's consort. The Mishti-khel, comprised Bhopal's most loyal commanders, including Bakshi Bahadur Mohammad Khan and his son Sardar Baqi Mohammad Khan (Umrao Doulah); and the Feroze-khel who settled in the neighbouring state of Kurwai.

(***The Begums of Bhopal,*** by Shaharyar Khan, page 238)

APPENDIX-2 : THE TREATY OF RAISEN, 1818

Treaty between the Honourable, the East India Company and the Nawab Nuzzur Mahomed Khan, Ruler of Bhopal, concluded by Captain Josiah Stewart on the part of The Honourable Company, in virtue of full powers granted by His Excellency The Marquis of Hastings, K.G., Governor-General, Etc., Etc., and by Kurrum Mahomed Khan Bahadur and Shahzad Musseeh Saheb on the part of the Nawab Nuzzur Mahomed Khan in virtue of full powers granted By The Nawab -1818.

APPENDIX-3 : THE FRENCH CONNECTION

Hakim Shahzad Masih played a very stabilising role in the governance of Bhopal. Hakim Shahzad Masih was the descendant of the Bourbon family from France. His great-grandfather Jean-Philippe de Bourbon, who claimed to be the natural-born son of King Charles III, known also as 'Connectable de Bourbon, was the first to arrive in India and reached Akbar's court. Jean-Phillip had married the granddaughter of King of France, Louis XI on 10 May 1505 CE. Jean-Philippe was forced to flee France in 1531 CE. After several adventures en route, he landed in India in 1547 CE and made his way to Delhi, during Akbar's reign. The Emperor was so impressed by this young man, that he was made a Nawab and appointed as Commander of the Artillery, with a task to reorganise it. The Bourbons prospered during the rule of the Mughals, but when their decline started, after Nadir Shah's raid on Delhi, Salvador de Bourbon was appointed by the Emperor as the Qilledar of Gwalior. During these turbulent times, the Fort was captured by the Marathas and the family was imprisoned in a dungeon. Fortunately, the British captured the Fort in 1740 CE. Having been set free, he opted to move on to Bhopal. Mamola Bai gave them shelter and a place to settle down in 1783 CE. In Bhopal, he was known as Inayat Masih. The loyalty of the Bourbon family to Bhopal was unquestionable and this debt was repaid over several generations.

Inayat Masih was an educated man, well versed in military tactics. His advice on matters military and security was regarded with great respect. He became a good friend and companion of Wazir Mohammad. However, he died in 1817 CE and that left his son

APPENDIX-8 : A LIST OF MONUMENTS COVERED IN THE BOOK

Sr. No.	Monuments	Period
1	Bhimbetka Rock Shelters	Prior to 1708 CE
2	Sanchi Stupa	
3	Mauryan Pillar in Bhopal	
4	Udayagiri Caves	
5	Bhojpur Shiva Temple	
6	Bhootnath Group of Temples, Ashapuri	
7	Bada Talab	
8	Mata Mandir and Ghat	
9	Mandir Shree Ji Ka	
10	Garhi Khanugaon	
11	Mangal Garh Fort	
12	Raisen Fort	
13	Hoshangabad Fort	
14	Ichhawar Fort	
15	Kurwai Fort	
16	Ginnorgarh Fort and Its Monuments	
17	Rani Kamlapati Palace	
18	Jagadishpur Fort	1709-1728 CE
19	Kadimi Hammam	
20	Fatehgarh Fort & Gate of Dost Mohammad Khan	
22	Dhai Seedi ki Masjid	
23	Tomb of Sardar Dost Mohommad Khan	
24	Masjid Yar Mohommah Khan	1728-1743 CE
25	Tomb of Nawab Yar Mohommad Khan	
26	Masjid Maji Sahiba (Retghat)	
27	Masjid Maji Sahiba (Kalan)	
28	Masjid Qudsia Begum	
29	Dargah Faiz Bahadur	1744-1777 CE
30	Masjid Hussain Bakshi	1777-1807 CE
31	Chhota Talab and Pul Pukhta	
32	Gangaurwali Baoli	
33	Baolis and Baradaris (Bagh Umrao Dulha)	1816-1819 CE

34	Bada Bagh and Baoli	1819-1837 CE
35	Aish Bagh and Baoli	
36	Gauhar Mahal	
37	Masjid Noor	
38	St. Francis of Assisi Cathedral	
39	Lal Darwaja	
40	Jama Masjid	
41	Adinath Digambar Jain Mandir	
42	Shwetambar Jain Mandir	
43	Masjid Toshakhana	
44	Pushpa Nagar Baoli	
45	Chhatri of Raja Khushwant Rai Saxena	
46	Palace of Jehangir Mohammad Khan (Police Headquarters)	1837-1844 CE
47	Moti Mahal Palace	1844-1868 CE
48	Moti Mahal Gate	
49	Moti Masjid	
50	Khirni Wala Maidan or Iqbal Maidan	
51	Jehangiria Higher Secondary School	
52	Bagh Farhat Afza	
53	Masjid Umrao Dulha	
54	Masjid Saifi	
55	Mandir Kamali	
56	Taj Mahal Palace	1868-1901 CE
57	Lal Masjid	
58	Noor Mahal	
59	Motia Talab, Noor Mahal Talab and Hussain Bakshi ki Tallaiya	
60	Yateem Khana	
61	Taj-Ul-Masajid	
62	Idgah	
63	Alexandria School	
64	Benazir Palace	
65	Pari Bazaar (Parween Manzil)	
66	Gulshan-e-Alam (Gol Ghar)	
67	Gates of ShahJehan Begum	

68	Bab-e-Karbala Gate	1868-1901 CE
69	Police Gate	
70	Bab-e-Ali Gate	
71	Military Gate	
72	Shaukat Mahal	
73	Zeenat Mahal	
74	Sheesh Mahal	
75	Sadar Manzil	
76	Hamid Manzil	
77	Maqbara Nawab Siddique Hassan	
78	Sultania Jenana Hospital	
79	Baradari at Shamla Hills	
80	Lal Kothi (Raj Bhawan)	
81	Ahmedabad Palace (Qasr-e-Sultani)	1901-1926 CE
82	Chief Minister's House	
83	Jehan Numa Palace	
84	Humayun Manzil	
85	Prince of Wales Hospital (Hamidia Hospital)	
86	Sulemania School	
87	Old Hamidia Library (Lokayukta Bhavan)	
88	The Imperial Bank	
89	Putli Ghar	
90	Bagh Hayat Afza	
91	Minto Hall	
92	Edward Museum (Central Library)	
93	Yacht Club	
94	Laxmi Talkies	
95	Noor-Us-Sabah	1926-1960 CE
96	Chiklod Kothi	
97	Cambridge School	
98	Royal Market	
99	Sophia Masjid	
100	Imperial Sabre	

BIBLIOGRAPHY

1. A Historical Sketch of Native Indian States in India in Subsidiary Alliance with the British, by G. B. Malleson, (1875).
2. A Brief History of the Bhopal Principality in Central India by W. Hough (1845).
3. A Memoir of Central India, including Malwa and Adjoining Provinces (Vol. 1) by S. J. Malcolm (1824).
4. An Account of My Life, by HH Nawab Sultan Jahan Begum,1912 Asr-i-Jadid, by Muhammad Amin Zuberi, 1929.
5. Beete Din Bhopal Ke (Urdu) by Khalid Muhammad Khan Begums of Bhopal, by Professor Claudia Preckel.
6. Bharatiya Digamber Jain Abhilekh Aur Tirth Parichay. (Hindi) Madhya Pradesh. by Kasturchand Jain. "Suman".
7. Bhopal Darpan (Hindi), Edited by Dr Razia Hamid and Dr Raft Sultan.
8. Bhopal in 1937-38, issued by Publicity Officer, State of Bhopal.
9. Bhopal Past and Present, by Dr. Syed Ashfaq Ali, Bhopal, 1969.
10. Bhopal State Gazetteer, by C.E. Luard and Kudrat Ali (1908), Reissued by INTACH, 2018.
11. Bhopal Beyond The Lakes: A Journey through time (n.d.).
12. BRIEF HISTORY OF THE DISTRICT BHOPAL (2023, April 10).
13. Chun Operation, Kashmir War by 4/16 Punjab by Lieutenant Colonel Muhammad Shahbaz, TI(M), Reid.
14. Hayat-i-Qudsi (English), Life of Nawab Gauhar Begum by Sultan Jahan Begum, 1918.
15. Hayat-e-ShahJehani (English), 1926, by Nawab Sultan Jahan Begum.
16. Historical Record of 4 Battalion 16" Punjab Regiment. by Officers of the Regiment (1932).
17. History of the Mahrattas (Vol. I) by J. G. Duff (1878).

18. History of Bhopal State by Kamala Mittal.
19. History Today, by 1.M. Brereton.
20. Hayat-e-Sahjehani by N. S. Begum (2018).
21. History of the Political and Military Transactions in India During the Administration of the Marquess of Hastings 1813-1823 (Vol. 1) by H. Prinsep (1825).
22. Indian Princes by M.Griffith.
23. Integration of Indian States by VP Menon.
24. Jang-e-Azadi aur Musalman (Hindi), by Khalid Mohammad Khan.
25. Later Mughals by W. Irvine (1996).
26. Life of Amir Khan by H. Prinsep (1832).
27. Memorials of service in India: from the correspondence of the late Major Samuel Charters MacPherson, C.B. by W. Macpherson (1865).
28. Memoirs of the Life of the Right Hon. Warren Hastings, First Governor-General of Bengal: Compiled from Original Papers II by G. R. Gleig (1841).
29. Narratives of Events regarding the Mutiny in India of 1857-58 and the Restoration or Authority (Vol. 1) (1881).
30. Nawab Hamidullah Khan (n.d.) [Read here](https://governor.mp.gov.in/hamid.aspx).
31. Official History of Indian Armed Forces 1971, by Shri 5.N. Prasad and others.
32. Official History of the Indian Armed Forces in the Second World War, by B Prasad and others.
33. Personal Diary of Lieutenant Colonel C.F. Dobbie.
34. Painted rock shelters at Lalghati area (n.d.) [Read here](http://nmma.nic.in/nmma/builtDetail.do?refId=2354&state=23).
35. Rock Art Heritage in Madhya Pradesh: A Special reference to IGRMS by K. S. P. Sankara Rao (2017).
36. Rani Kamlapati Bhopal: शौर्य और सौंदर्य की प्रतिमूर्ति थीं रानीकमलापति, जिनके नाम पर हुआ हबीबगंज रेलवेस्टेशन by RAVINDRA SONI (2021, November 13)
37. Rock paintings facing threat of going into oblivion by S. Bhadoria (2020, January 10).

38. Roznamcha (Dost's Diary)-(Persian).
39. Solah Punjab, The History of the 16" Punjab Regiment by Lieutenant Colonel IP Lawford, MC and Major W.E. Catto.
40. Seir-ul-Mutaqherin by S.-G. Hossein-Khan (1926).
41. Taj-ul-Iqbal, Tarikh Bhopal, by Her Highness Nawab Shahjehan Begum Nawab of Bhopal (1876.)
42. Tazkira-I-Baqi. A Short Biography of Umrao Dulha, Nawab Baqi Mohammad Khan Sahib Bahadur, Nasrat Jung, by Her Highness Sultan Jahan Begum, Translated by Captain Nawada Rashiduzzafar Khan (1927), reprint in 2016.
43. The Armies of India, by Lieutenant General Sir George Fletcher Macmunn.
44. The Archaeology of Bhopal Region by R. K. Sharma & R. Ali (1980.)
45. The Begums of Bhopal, by Shaharyar M Khan.
46. The Bourbons and Begums of Bhopal, by Indira Iyengar, 2018.
47. The Deceivers: Allied Military Deception in the Second World War, by Thaddeus Holt.
48. The Early Years of East India Company's Armies to c 1800, by GI Bryant.
49. The History of the 4 Indian Infantry Division, by Carl Titterington.
50. Talash-e-Bhopal.
51. The Maharaja's Paltans (History of Indian State Forces 1888-1948 by Richard Head and Tony McClenaghan.
52. The táj-ulikbál tarikh Bhopal, or, The history of Bhopal by Nawab ShahJehan Begum (1876).
53. The History of India, as Told by Its Own Historians: The Mohammadan Period (Vol. 8) by H. M. Elliot (1877).
54. The History of India: As Told by its Own Historians. The Mohammadan Period VII (Vol. 7) by H. M. Elliot (1966).
55. The Royal Journey of Bhopal by S. A. Husain (2007).
56. Vintage Bhopal, by Gita Subherwal& Ashok Shah.
57. रानीकमलापति का जीवनपरिचय व इतिहास (Bio) by Bio4hindi (2021, December 26)

END NOTES

1 . Atal Bihari Vajpayee Institute of Good Governance and Policy Analysis. Bhopal Beyond the lakes: A journey through time. 20.

2 . P. Sankara Rao, K. Seshadri and Sarit Kumar Chaudhuri. Rock Art Heritage in Madhya Pradesh: A Special Reference to IGRMS. (Rock art of Central India with Special Reference to Madhya Pradesh, Bhopal, December 2017).

3 . https://reflectionsofindia.com/2014/09/27/environmentalbhopal/img_0536rockartres/

4 . https://www.thehitavada.com/Encyc/2020/1/10/Rock-paintings-facing-threat-of-going-into-oblivion.html

5 . http://nmma.nic.in/nmma/builtDetail.do?refId=2354&state=23

6 . Sharma R. K and Rahman Ali. The Archaeology of Bhopal Region. (Delhi: Agam Kala Prakashan, 1980).

7 . Shāhjahān Begum. The táj-ulikbáltárikh Bhopal, or, The history of Bhopal. Translated by Barstow, H. C. (Calcutta: Thacker, Spink and Co., 1876). 222.

8 . André Wink, Al-Hind, the Making of the Indo-Islamic World (Germany: E.J. Brill, 1991), 152.

9 . https://bhopal.nic.in/en/history/#:~:text=%E2%80%9CThe%20name%20(Bhopal)%20is,attributed%20to%20this%20monarch%20himself.

10 . https://timesofindia.indiatimes.com/city/bhopal/rani-kamlapati-things-you-must-know-about-the-gond-queen/articleshow/87708526.cms

11 . https://bio4hindi.blogspot.com/2021/12/rani-kamlapati-biography-in-hindi.html

12 . Naidu, M. (2021). Nizaam-I-Bhopal: Militaries of Bhopal State : a Historical Review. Vij Books India Pvt. Limited. 16-17

13 . https://whc.unesco.org/en/list/925/

14 . https://www.britannica.com/place/Bhimbetka-rock-shelters

15 . https://www.mptourism.com/destination-bhimbetka.php

16 . https://en.wikipedia.org/wiki/Bhimbetka_rock_shelters

17 . https://en.wikipedia.org/wiki/Sanchi

18 . https://www.britannica.com/place/Great-Stupa-Buddhist-monument-Sanchi-India

19 . https://www.britannica.com/place/Sanchi-historical-site-India

20 . https://whc.unesco.org/en/list/524/

21 . https://whc.unesco.org/en/list/524/

22 . https://vidisha.nic.in/en/tourist-place/udaigiri-cave/

23 . https://timesofindia.indiatimes.com/travel/destinations/all-you-need-to-know-about-the-rock-cut-caves-of-udayagiri-madhya-pradesh/articleshow/93542172.cms

24 . https://www.mptourism.com/bhojpur-ancient-shiva-temple-near-bhopal.html

25 . https://www.wmf.org/blog/solving-riddles-temples-ashapuri-madhya-pradesh-india

26 . https://en.wikipedia.org/wiki/Bhojtal

27 . Syed Akhtar Husain. The Royal Journey of Bhopal. (Bhopal: Oriental Scientific Publishing Co., 2007). 2

28 . https://en.wikipedia.org/wiki/Mangalgarh,_Bhopal

29 . https://raisen.nic.in/en/history/

30 . Luard, C. E. (2018). Bhopal State Gazetteer. Manjul Publishing House. 111-115

31 . https://raisen.nic.in/en/culture-heritage/
32 . https://dsal.uchicago.edu/reference/gazetteer/pager.html?objectid=DS405.1.I34_V13_330.gif
33 . https://www.royalark.net/India2/kurwai.htm
34 . https://en.wikipedia.org/wiki/Kurwai_State#:~:text=2%20See%20also-,History,the%20Third%20Anglo%2DMaratha%20War.
35 . https://dsal.uchicago.edu/reference/gazetteer/pager.html?objectid=DS405.1.I34_V15_412.gif
36 . https://bansalnews.com/kurwai-state-fort-nawab-zafar-ali-khan-still-lives-in-kurwai-fort-of-madhya-pradesh-vkj/
37 . https://en.wikipedia.org/wiki/Kurwai_State#:~:text=2%20See%20also-,History,the%20Third%20Anglo%2DMaratha%20War.
38 . https://en.wikipedia.org/wiki/Shahryar_Khan
39 . https://www.impriindia.com/insights/rani-kamalapati-ginnorgarh-fort/
40 . Tourism Department Opportunities at Ratapani Sanctuary, INTACH Bhopal Report, 2021
41 . https://dbpedia.org/page/Ginnorgarh
42 . Luard, C. E. (2018). Bhopal State Gazetteer. Manjul Publishing House. 10
43 . Naidu, M. (2021). Nizaam-I-Bhopal: Militaries of Bhopal State : a Historical Review. Vij Books India Pvt. Limited. 12
44 . William Irvine. Later Mughals. (India: Munshiram Manoharlal, 1996). 1-28.
45 . Henry Miers, Elliot. The History of India: As Told by Its Own Historians. The Muhammadan Period VII. (AMS Press, 1966. 487-89 and 490-92.
46 . James Grant Duff. History of the Mahrattas Vol I. (Bombay: Times of India Office, 1878).396.
47 . Seid-Gholam Hossein-Khan. Seir-ul-Mutaqherin Vol I. (Delhi: Low Price Publications, 1926).162.
48 . Henry Miers Elliot. The History of India, as Told by Its Own Historians: The Muhammadan Period Vol 8. (United Kingdom: Trübner and Company, 1869). 57.
49 . Bhopal: The Built Heritage, INTACH Bhopal, 2005 (Unpublished)
50 . Naidu, M. (2021). Nizaam-I-Bhopal: Militaries of Bhopal State : a Historical Review. Vij Books India Pvt. Limited. 17
51 . Naidu, M. (2021). Nizaam-I-Bhopal: Militaries of Bhopal State : a Historical Review. Vij Books India Pvt. Limited. 18
52 . The Taj-ul Ikbal Tarikh Bhopal Or The History of Bhopal. (2020). Indian National Trust for Art and Cultural Heritage (INTACH). 227-228
53 . Sultan Jahan Begum. (2018). Hayat-i-Shahjehani: Life of Her Highness the Late Nawab Shahjehan Begum of Bhopal. INTACH.117,293
54 . https://www.hindustantimes.com/bhopal/bhopal-communal-clashes-a-heritage-gate-is-what-caused-hindu-muslim-tensions/story-L3mnuzoaH7n0NrrfFAVCoJ.html
55 . Architectural Conservation, Documentation and study of Gates of Bhopal, Intach Bhopal and Department of Architecture and Planning, MANIT Bhopal. 2018
56 . Naidu, M. (2021). Nizaam-I-Bhopal: Militaries of Bhopal State : a Historical Review. Vij Books India Pvt. Limited. 18
57 . ePGPathshala, Indian Culture, SCHI, 25
58 . Archaeology, Archives and Museums, Madhya Pradesh Bhopal
59 . Grant Duff. History of MarathasVol I. 458.
60 . Sir John Malcolm. A Memoir of Central India, Including Malwa and Adjoining provinces Vol I. (London: Kingsbury, Parbury& Allen, Leadenhall-Street, 1824) 230
61 . Elliot. The History of India, as Told by Its Own Historians: The Muhammadan Period Vol 8. 58 and 69.

62 . Malhotra, O. P. (2015). Rise and Establishment of Bhopal State: From Its Foundation to 1819 A.D. Indra Publishing House. 81
63 . Malhotra, O. P. (2015). Rise and Establishment of Bhopal State: From Its Foundation to 1819 A.D. Indra Publishing House. 85
64 . Bhopal: The Built Heritage, INTACH Bhopal, 2005 (Unpublished)
65 . Bhopal: The Built Heritage, INTACH Bhopal, 2005 (Unpublished)
66 . Bhopal: The Built Heritage, INTACH Bhopal, 2005 (Unpublished)
67 . Rav Bahadur Ganesh Chimaji Vad. D.B. Parasnis. Selections from the Satara rajas and The Peswas Diaries III, Vol 1. (Poona: The Deccan Vanacular Translation Society, 1907) 14 and 51.
68 . Malcom. Central India, I. 293-5.
69 . Bhopal: The Built Heritage, INTACH Bhopal, 2005 (Unpublished)
70 . Duff. History of MarathasVol II. 40.
71 . George Robert Gleig. Memoirs of the Life of the Right Hon. Warren Hastings, First Governor-General of Bengal: Compiled from Original Papers II. (United Kingdom: R. Bentley, 1841). 196 and 217.
72 . Duff. The history of Marathas II. 98.
73 . University of Calcutta. The Calcutta Review, Vol. 26. (Serampore: Calcutta University Press, 1856) 557.
74 . Life of Amir Khan, 29
75 . Life of Amir Khan, 41
76 . Bhopal: The Built Heritage, INTACH Bhopal, 2005 (Unpublished)
77 . ePGPathshala, Indian Culture, SCHI, 25
78 . Bhopal: The Built Heritage, INTACH Bhopal, 2005 (Unpublished)
79 . Bhopal: The Built Heritage, INTACH Bhopal, 2005 (Unpublished)
80 . Malcom, Central India I, 322.
81 . Malcom, Central India I, 335.
82 . H.T. Prinsep. History of the Political and Military Transactions in India During the Administration of the Marquess of Hastings 1813-1823 Vol. I. (London: Kingsbury, Parbury& Allen, 1825). 233.
83 . Princep, Hastings I, 256.
84 . Malcom, Central India I, 336.
85 . Princep, Hastings I, 343.
86 . H.T. Prinsep. History of the Political and Military Transactions in India During the Administration of the Marquess of Hastings 1813-1823 Vol. I. (London: Kingsbury, Parbury& Allen, 1825). 149.
87 . Bhopal: The Built Heritage, INTACH Bhopal, 2005 (Unpublished)
88 . Bhopal: The Built Heritage, INTACH Bhopal, 2005 (Unpublished)
89 . The Taj-ul Ikbal Tarikh Bhopal Or The History of Bhopal. (2020). Indian National Trust for Art and Cultural Heritage (INTACH).225
90 . Sultan Jahan, B. (1918). Hayat-i-Qudsi (W. S. Davis, Trans.). Kegan Paul, Trench, Trubner& Co. Ltd. 133
91 . Bhopal: The Built Heritage, INTACH Bhopal, 2005 (Unpublished)
92 . Bhopal: The Built Heritage, INTACH Bhopal, 2005 (Unpublished)
93 . Bhopal: The Built Heritage, INTACH Bhopal, 2005 (Unpublished)
94 . Bhopal: The Built Heritage, INTACH Bhopal, 2005 (Unpublished)
95 . Architectural Conservation, Documentation and study of Gates of Bhopal, Intach Bhopal and Department of Architecture and Planning, MANIT Bhopal. 2018
96 . Sultan Jahan, B. (1918). Hayat-i-Qudsi (W. S. Davis, Trans.). Kegan Paul, Trench, Trubner& Co. Ltd. 134
97 . ePGPathshala, Indian Culture, SCHI, 25

98 . Sultan Jahan, B. (1918). Hayat-i-Qudsi (W. S. Davis, Trans.). Kegan Paul, Trench, Trubner& Co. Ltd. 134
99 . Sultan Jahan, B. (1918). Hayat-i-Qudsi (W. S. Davis, Trans.). Kegan Paul, Trench, Trubner& Co. Ltd. 134
100 . Luard, C. E. (2018). Bhopal State Gazetteer. Manjul Publishing House. 96
101 . Bhopal: The Built Heritage, INTACH Bhopal, 2005 (Unpublished)
102 . Bhopal: The Built Heritage, INTACH Bhopal, 2005 (Unpublished)
103 . Bhopal: The Built Heritage, INTACH Bhopal, 2005 (Unpublished)
104 . Bhopal: The Built Heritage, INTACH Bhopal, 2005 (Unpublished)
105 . Bhopal: The Built Heritage, INTACH Bhopal, 2005 (Unpublished)
106 . ePGPathshala, Indian Culture, SCHI, 25
107 . William Macpherson. Memorials of service in India: from the correspondence of the late Major Samuel Charters MacPherson, C.B. (London: John Murray, Alemarle Street, 1865)
108 . Narratives of Events regarding the Mutiny in India of 1857-58 and the Restoration or Authority, Vol. I (Calcutta, Foreign Department Press, 1881).
109 . Bhopal: The Built Heritage, INTACH Bhopal, 2005 (Unpublished)
110 . Architectural Conservation, Documentation and study of Gates of Bhopal, Intach Bhopal and Department of Architecture and Planning, MANIT Bhopal. 2018
111 . The Taj-ul Ikbal Tarikh Bhopal Or The History of Bhopal. (2020). Indian National Trust for Art and Cultural Heritage (INTACH). 227
112 . The Taj-ul Ikbal Tarikh Bhopal Or The History of Bhopal. (2020). Indian National Trust for Art and Cultural Heritage (INTACH). 226
113 . Bhopal: The Built Heritage, INTACH Bhopal, 2005 (Unpublished)
114 . Bhopal: The Built Heritage, INTACH Bhopal, 2005 (Unpublished)
115 . Bhopal: The Built Heritage, INTACH Bhopal, 2005 (Unpublished)
116 . Bhopal: The Built Heritage, INTACH Bhopal, 2005 (Unpublished)
117 . Bhopal: The Built Heritage, INTACH Bhopal, 2005 (Unpublished)
118 . Bhopal: The Built Heritage, INTACH Bhopal, 2005 (Unpublished)
119 . ePGPathshala, Indian Culture, SCHI, 25
120 . Bhopal: The Built Heritage, INTACH Bhopal, 2005 (Unpublished)
121 . Bhopal: The Built Heritage, INTACH Bhopal, 2005 (Unpublished)
122 . Naidu, M. (2021). Nizaam-I-Bhopal: Militaries of Bhopal State : a Historical Review. Vij Books India Pvt. Limited. 258
123 . Architectural Conservation, Documentation and study of Gates of Bhopal, Intach Bhopal and Department of Architecture and Planning, MANIT Bhopal. 2018
124 . Architectural Conservation, Documentation and study of Gates of Bhopal, Intach Bhopal and Department of Architecture and Planning, MANIT Bhopal. 2018
125 . Architectural Conservation, Documentation and study of Gates of Bhopal, Intach Bhopal and Department of Architecture and Planning, MANIT Bhopal. 2018
126 . Architectural Conservation, Documentation and study of Gates of Bhopal, Intach Bhopal and Department of Architecture and Planning, MANIT Bhopal. 2018
127 . Bhopal: The Built Heritage, INTACH Bhopal, 2005 (Unpublished)
128 . Bhopal: The Built Heritage, INTACH Bhopal, 2005 (Unpublished)
129 . Bhopal: The Built Heritage, INTACH Bhopal, 2005 (Unpublished)
130 . DPR- Restoration and conservation proposal of Sulemania School, INTACH
131 . https://governor.mp.gov.in/Commis_Period.aspx
132 . Bhopal: The Built Heritage, INTACH Bhopal, 2005 (Unpublished)
133 . *The Taj-ul Ikbal Tarikh Bhopal Or The History of Bhopal. (2020).* Indian National Trust for Art and Cultural Heritage (INTACH).
134 . Patnaik, M. (2013). Anchoring Heritage With History - Minto Hall (Bhopal, India)).

Preservation Education and Research, 6, 73-87.

135 . https://web.archive.org/web/20150607125302/http://members.iinet.net.au/~royalty/ips/b/bhopal.html

136 . https://web.archive.org/web/20200126161312/http://www.muslimissues.com/

137 . https://governor.mp.gov.in/hamid.aspx

138 . https://governor.mp.gov.in/hamid.aspx

139 . Khan, K. M. (2014). *Beete Din Bhopal Ke.* Shahid Mohammad Khan, Bhopal. 434

140 . https://hotelimperialsabre.co.in/about-us/

141 . Luard, C. E. (2018). Bhopal State Gazetteer. Manjul Publishing House. 16

142 Naidu, M. (2021). *Nizaam-I-Bhopal: Militaries of Bhopal State : a Historical Review.* Vij Books India Pvt. Limited. 100

143 . Luard, C. E. (2018). *Bhopal State Gazetteer.* Manjul Publishing House. 32

144 . Naidu, M. (2021). *Nizaam-I-Bhopal: Militaries of Bhopal State : a Historical Review.* Vij Books India Pvt. Limited. 107

145 . Naidu, M. (2021). *Nizaam-I-Bhopal: Militaries of Bhopal State : a Historical Review.* Vij Books India Pvt. Limited. 118

146 . Naidu, M. (2021). *Nizaam-I-Bhopal: Militaries of Bhopal State : a Historical Review.* Vij Books India Pvt. Limited. 120

147 . Sultan Jahan Begum. (2018). *Hayat-i-Shahjehani: Life of Her Highness the Late Nawab Shahjehan Begum of Bhopal.* INTACH. 28

148 . Naidu, M. (2021). *Nizaam-I-Bhopal: Militaries of Bhopal State : a Historical Review.* Vij Books India Pvt. Limited.273

149 . Sultan Jahan Begum. (2018). *Hayat-i-Shahjehani: Life of Her Highness the Late Nawab Shahjehan Begum of Bhopal.* INTACH. 281

150 . Sultan Jahan Begum. (2018). *Hayat-i-Shahjehani: Life of Her Highness the Late Nawab Shahjehan Begum of Bhopal.* INTACH. 57-58

151 . https://timesofindia.indiatimes.com/life-style/spotlight/beyond-bhimbetka-explore-the-cave-art-of-bhopal/articleshow/68424058.cms

152 . Luard, C. E. (2018). *Bhopal State Gazetteer.* Manjul Publishing House. 95-100

153 . Luard, C. E. (2018). *Bhopal State Gazetteer.* Manjul Publishing House. 97

154 . Naidu, M. (2021). *Nizaam-I-Bhopal: Militaries of Bhopal State : a Historical Review.* Vij Books India Pvt. Limited. 44-45

155 . Atal Bihari Vajpayee Institute of Good Governance and Policy Analysis. Bhopal Beyond the lakes: A journey through time. 20.

156 . P. Sankara Rao, K. Seshadri and Sarit Kumar Chaudhuri. Rock Art Heritage in Madhya Pradesh: A Special Reference to IGRMS. (Rock art of Central India with Special Reference to Madhya Pradesh, Bhopal, December 2017).

157 . https://reflectionsofindia.com/2014/09/27/environmentalbhopal/img_0536rockartres/

158 . https://www.thehitavada.com/Encyc/2020/1/10/Rock-paintings-facing-threat-of-going-into-oblivion.html

159 . http://nmma.nic.in/nmma/builtDetail.do?refId=2354&state=23

160 . Sharma R. K and Rahman Ali. The Archaeology of Bhopal Region. (Delhi: Agam Kala Prakashan, 1980).

REFERENCES OF IMAGES

- Bhimbetka Rock Shelters
  https://www.mptourism.com/destination-bhimbetka.php
- Sanchi
  https://www.mptourism.com/destination-sanchi.php
- Mauryan Pillar
  INTACH Bhopal
- Udayagiri Caves
  https://www.worldhistory.org/img/r/p/1500x1500/3878.jpg.webp?v=1626538503
- Bhojpur Shiva Temple
  https://en.wikipedia.org/wiki/Bhojeshwar_Temple#/media/File:Shiva_Temple,_Bhojpur_01.jpg
- Ashapuri Temple
  Raghav Sharma
- Bada Talab
  https://images.bhaskarassets.com/web2images/521/2021/07/20/whatsapp-image-2021-07-20-at-125148-pm_1626765803.jpeg
- Mangal Garh Fort
  https://content.jdmagicbox.com/comp/bhopal/n4/0755px755.x755.180629230131.n9n4/catalogue/fort-mangalgarh-mangal-garh-bhopal-lh6bfikeos.jpg?clr=#382e2e
- Raisen Fort
  https://navbharattimes.indiatimes.com/thumb/96826925/facts-about-raisen-fort-madhya-pradesh-96826925.jpg?imgsize=185236&width=1200&height=900&resizemode=75
- Hoshangabad Fort
  https://i.ytimg.com/vi/UTmCnyJKesY/maxresdefault.jpg
- Kurwai Fort
  https://i.ytimg.com/vi/pM4h2Edqt9w/maxresdefault.jpg
- Hawa Mahal, Ginnorgarh Fort
  INTACH Bhopal
- Rani Kamlapati Palace
  INTACH Bhopal
- Image of Dost Mohammad Khan
  Taha Pasha
- Jagadishpur Fort
  Raghav Sharma
- Fatehgarh Fort
  INTACH Bhopal

- Dhai Seedi ki Masjid
  https://madainproject.com/content/media/collect/dhai_seedhi_masjid_66736.jpg

- Tomb of Sardar Dost Mohammad Khan
  INTACH Bhopal

- Image of Bhopal State Insignia
  https://upload.wikimedia.org/wikipedia/commons/1/1a/CoA_Bhopal.png

- Tomb of Nawab Yar Mohammad Khan
  https://www.google.com/maps/place/Makbara+of+Hayat+Mohd+Khan/@23.3584418,77.4194116,3a,75y/data=!3m8!1e2!3m6!1sAF1QipNZM-mQ7a1TsgbENnG2TL-3JKrVRC3U4K1QHng6G!2e10!3e12!6shttps:%2F%2Flh5.googleusercontent.com%2Fp%2FAF1QipNZM-mQ7a1TsgbENnG2TL3JKrVRC3U4K1QHng6G%3Dw203-h152-k-no!7i4608!8i3456!4m7!3m6!1s0x397c6f7a9ed5a86b:0x-da6aa1a90dce097f!8m2!3d23.3584676!4d77.4194114!10e5! 16s%2Fg%2F11lkx3zp-gl?entry=ttu

- Masjid Maji Sahiba (Retghat)
  INTACH Bhopal

- Dargah Faiz Bahadur
  INTACH Bhopal

- Chhota Talab and Pul Pukhta
  INTACH Bhopal

- Image of Nawab Nazar Mohammad Khan
  Taha Pasha

- Image of Nawab Qudsia Begum
  Taha Pasha

- Bada Bagh and Baoli
  https://www.shutterstock.com/preview/8819332e/00fff18f/Shutterstock_8819332e.jpg

- Gauhar Mahal
  https://kevinstandagephotography.files.wordpress.com/2018/12/ksp_6086.jpg

- St. Francis of Assisi Cathedral
  https://pbs.twimg.com/media/E24gVlMVgAAtckx.jpg

- Jama Masjid
  https://lh5.googleusercontent.com/-52btl8hwewI/WHj_LUGFg9I/AAAAAAAAlYg/zTLZW22_JxcLii3irkDD8je1wz6L6i7UQCLIB/photo.jpg

- Adinath Digambar Jain Mandir
  INTACH Bhopal

- Shwetambar Jain Mandir
  INTACH Bhopal

- Chhatri of Raja Khushwant Rai Saxena
  INTACH Bhopal

- Palace of Jehangir Mohammad Khan
  INTACH Bhopal

- Image of Nawab Sikandar Jahan Begum
  https://blogs.soas.ac.uk/archives/2020/03/08/sikandar_begum_nawab_of_bhopal/

- Moti Mahal Palace
  INTACH Bhopal

- Moti Mahal Gate
  INTACH Bhopal

- Moti Masjid
  INTACH Bhopal

- Khirni Wala Maidan (Iqbal Maidan)
  https://mapio.net/images-p/16017374.jpg

- Jehangiria Higher Secondary School
  INTACH Bhopal

- Image of Nawab ShahJehan Begum
  Taha Pasha

- Taj Mahal Palace
  https://www.reddit.com/media?url=https%3A%2F%2Fi.redd.it%2Fdwtunc5blcc81.jpg&rdt=37541

- Lal Masjid
  https://upload.wikimedia.org/wikipedia/commons/thumb/1/1c/Inside_of_Masjid_Kulsoom_Bi%2C_Chaarbatti_Square%2C_Bhopal.jpg/1200px-Inside_of_Masjid_Kulsoom_Bi%2C_Chaarbatti_Square%2C_Bhopal.jpg

- Motia Talab, Noor Mahal Talab and Hussain Bakshi ki Tallaiya
  https://scontent.fbho1-2.fna.fbcdn.net/v/t1.6435-9/115750019_10157770482572582_6315032378824231888_n.jpg?_nc_cat=110&ccb=1-7&_nc_sid=dd63ad&_nc_ohc=SV3NS8NcoZcAX-kHZEh&_nc_ht=scontent.fbho1-2.fna&oh=00_AfCa4JzG0p_RQInlCgISPk1SjqV2eqbh_65bVhgiP7eJkw&oe=65F2C94B

- Taj-Ul-Masajid
  https://lemonicks.com/wp-content/uploads/2020/05/Bhopal-Tajulmasajid-20200315_104044.jpg

- Idgah
  https://www.google.com/maps/place/Idgah,+Bhopal+%D8%B9%DB%8C%D8%AF%DA%AF%D8%A7%DB%81+%D8%A8%DA%BE%D9%88%D9%BE%D8%A7%D9%84%E2%80%AD/@23.269642,77.3825562,3a,75y/data=!3m8!1e2!3m6!1sAF1QipN-PY6gkj3nosqN2dS0vYZK38jO3zzzBsbqYAMv!2e10!3e12!6shttps:%2F%2Flh5.googleusercontent.com%2Fp%2FAF1QipN-PY6gkj3nosqN2dS0vYZK38jO3zzzBsbqYAMv%3Dw203-h114-k-no!7i4160!8i2340!4m11!1m2!2m1!1sidgah!3m7!1s0x397c680bc2279483:0xdb94a59998895a6f!8m2!3d23.269642!4d77.3825562!10e5!15sCgVpZGdhaJIBFXJlbGlnaW91c19kZXN0aW5hdGlvbuABAA!16s%2Fg%2F12629mds3?entry=ttu

- Alexandria School
  INTACH Bhopal

- Benazir Palace
  https://images.bhaskarassets.com/web2images/521/2020/03/24/ab_1585001750.jpg

- Gulshan-e-Alam (Gol Ghar)
  Abhishek Goud

- Bab-e-Karbala Gate
  INTACH Bhopal

- Bab-e-Ali Gate
  INTACH Bhopal

- Military Gate
  INTACH Bhopal

- Shaukat Mahal
  https://studiosanchit.files.wordpress.com/2014/07/4.jpg

- Zeenat Mahal
  INTACH Bhopal

- Sheesh Mahal
  INTACH Bhopal

- Sadar Manzil
  INTACH Bhopal
- Hamid Manzil
  INTACH Bhopal

- Maqbara Nawab Siddique Hassan
  Raghav Sharma

- Baradari at Shamla Hills
  https://www.google.com/maps/place/Upper+Lake+secret+view+point/@23.240047,77.3797922,3485a,13.1y/data=!3m8!1e2!3m6!1sAF1QipOAPHqkCZUIZuY1pHwGb-zzD_-dJ1yJq8jJZGK8V!2e10!3e12!6shttps:%2F%2Flh5.googleusercontent.com%2F-p%2FAF1QipOAPHqkCZUIZuY1pHwGbzzD_-dJ1yJq8jJZGK8V%3Dw203-h440-k-no!7i1844!8i4000!4m7!3m6!1s0x397c431416eb2651:0xecb3539ebef91b8!8m2!3d23.240047!4d77.3797922!10e5!16s%2Fg%2F11stxpvg3s?entry=ttu

- Lal Kothi (Raj Bhawan)
  https://dynamic-media-cdn.tripadvisor.com/media/photo-o/1c/97/cd/c2/the-beautiful-raj-bhavan.jpg?w=1200&h=1200&s=1

- Image of Nawab Sultan Jahan Begum
  https://svasalife.com/the-begums-of-bhopal/

- Ahmedabad Palace
  INTACH Bhopal
- Chief Minister's House
  INTACH Bhopal

- Jehan Numa Palace
  https://gos3.ibcdn.com/c5bc8d0ca1db11ec86a40a58a9feac02.jpg

- Humayun Manzil
  INTACH Bhopal

- Prince of Wales Hospital (Hamidia Hospital)
  INTACH Bhopal

- Sulemania School
  INTACH Bhopal

- Old Hamidia Library (Lokayukta Bhavan)
  https://www.google.com/maps/place/Lokayukt+Bhavan/@23.2623991,77.3881845,3a,75y/data=!3m8!1e2!3m6!1sAF1QipOvRdX8zlKsi9f_siXdJTD9M_tl29d8iXd09MP-m!2e10!3e12!6shttps:%2F%2Flh5.googleusercontent.com%2Fp%2FAF1QipOvRdX-8zlKsi9f_siXdJTD9M_tl29d8iXd09MPm%3Dw203-h114-k-no!7i3264!8i1836!4m7!3m6!1s0x397c680571cd168d:0x2beb9b418fd1b716!8m2!3d23.2623991!4d77.3881845!10e5!16s%2Fg%2F124yndbxl?entry=ttu

- Minto Hall
  https://pbs.twimg.com/media/EjzsYypUwAENvLx.jpg

- Edward Museum (Central Library)
  https://images.bhaskarassets.com/thumb/1200x900/web2images/521/2019/07/18/0521_maulana_azad_central_library.jpg

- Image of Nawab Hamidullah Khan
  Taha Pasha

- Noor-Us-Sabah
  https://www.hoteldekho.com/storage/img/hotels/1639472742img10.jpg

- Chiklod Kothi
  INTACH Bhopal
- Sophia Masjid
  INTACH Bhopal

- Imperial Sabre
  https://hotelimperialsabre.co.in/wp-content/uploads/2021/10/Use12-scaled.jpg